A JOURNEY OF RICHES

Returning to Love

10 Insights to touch your soul!

A Journey Of Riches - Returning to Love

10 Insights to touch your soul! © 2020

Published by Motion Media International
Editing: Gwendolyn Parker, Chris Drabenstott, Suzie Davis, and Michele Cempaka
Cover Design: Motion Media International
Typesetting & Assembly: Motion Media International
Printing: Amazon and Ingram Sparks

Creator: John Spender - Primary Author
Title: *A Journey Of Riches - Returning to Love*
ISBN Digital: 978-1-925919-17-2
ISBN Print: 978-1-925919-18-9
Subjects: Self-Help, Motivation/Inspiration and Spirituality.

--- ❖ ---

Acknowledgments

Reading and writing is a gift that very few give to themselves. It is such a powerful way to reflect and gain closure from the past; reading and writing is a therapeutic process. The experience raises one's self-esteem, confidence, and awareness of self.

I learned this when I created the first book in the A Journey Of Riches series, which now includes twenty one books with over 220 different co-authors from forty different countries. It's not easy to write about your personal experiences and I honor and respect every one of the authors who have collaborated in the series thus far.

For many of the authors, English is their second language, which is a significant achievement in itself. In creating this anthology of short stories, I have been touched by the amount of generosity, gratitude, and shared energy that this experience has given everyone.

The inspiration for A Journey of Riches, Returning to Love came from my yearning to see more love in the world. Naturally, I could not have created this book without the nine other co-authors who all said YES when I asked them to share their insights and wisdom. Just as each chapter in this book makes for inspiring reading, each story represents one chapter in the life of each of the authors, with the chief aim of having you, the reader, living a more inspired life. Together we can share more love with the world.

I want to thank all the authors for entrusting me with their unique memories, encounters, and wisdom. Thank you for sharing and opening the door to your soul so that others may learn from your experience. I trust the readers will gain confidence from your successes, and also wisdom, from your failures.

I also want to thank my family. I know you are proud of me, seeing how far I have come from that 10-year-old boy who was learning how to read and write at a basic level. Big shout out to my Mom, Robert, Dad, Merril; my brother Adam and his daughter Krystal; my sister Hollie, her partner Brian, my nephew Charlie and niece, Heidi; thank you for your support. Also, kudos to my grandparents, Gran and Pop, who are alive and well, and Ma and Pa, who now rest in peace. They accept me just the way I am with all my travels and adventures around the world.

Thanks to all the team at Motion Media International; you have done an excellent job at editing and collating this book. It was a pleasure working with you on this successful project, and I thank you for your patience in dealing with the various changes and adjustments along the way.

Thank you, the reader, for having the courage to look at your life and how you can improve your future in a fast and rapidly changing world.

Thank you again to my fellow co-authors: Julie Williams, Lilibeth Ranchez, Robin Seeger, Suzanne Rushton, Marie Crawford, Debi Beebe, Ryan Doherty, Annie Pearson, and Mia Paul.

We would greatly appreciate an honest review on Amazon! This is how we gain more readers to our inspiring book!

With gratitude
John Spender

Praise for A Journey of Riches book series

"The A Journey of Riches book series is a great collection of inspiring short stories that will leave you wanting more!"
~ Alex Hoffmann, Network Marketing Guru.

"If you are looking for an inspiring read to get you through any change, this is it!! This book is comprised of many gripping perspectives from a collection of successful international authors with a tone of wisdom to share."
~ Theera Phetmalaigul, Entrepreneur/Investor.

"*A Journey of Riches* is an empowering series that implements two simple words in overcoming life's struggles.

By diving into the meaning of the words "problem" and "challenge," you will find yourself motivated to believe in the triumph of perseverance. With many different authors from all around the world coming together to share various stories of life's trials, you will find yourself drenched in encouragement to push through even the darkest of battles.

The stories are heartfelt personal shares of moving through and transforming challenges into rich life experiences.

The book will move, touch and inspire your spirit to face and overcome any of life's adversities. It is a truly inspirational read. Thank you for being the kind open soul you are, John!!"
~ Casey Plouffe, Seven Figure Network Marketer.

"A must-read for anyone facing major changes or challenges in life right now. This book will give you the courage to move through any struggle with confidence, grace, and ease."
~ Jo-Anne Irwin - Transformational Coach and Best Selling Author.

"I have enjoyed the *Journey of Riches* book series. Each person's story is written from the heart, and everyone's journey is different. We all have a story to tell, and John Spender does an amazing job of finding authors, and combining their stories into uplifting books."
~ Liz Misner Palmer, Foreign Service Officer.

"A timely read as I'm facing a few challenges right now. I like the various insights from the different

authors. This book will inspire you to move through any challenge or change that you are experiencing."
~ David Ostrand, Business Owner.

"I've known John Spender for a while now, and I was blessed with an opportunity to be in book four in the series. I know that you will enjoy this new journey like the rest of the books in the series. The collection of stories will assist you with making changes, dealing with challenges, and seeing that transformation is possible for your life."
~ Charlie O' Shea, Entrepreneur.

"A *Journey of Riches* series will draw you in and help you dig deep into your soul. Authors have unbelievable life stories of purpose inside of them. John Spender is dedicated to bringing peace, love, and adventure to the world of his readers! Dive into this series, and you will be transformed!"
~ Jeana Matichak, Author of Finding Peace.

"Awesome! Truly inspirational! It is amazing what the human spirit can achieve and overcome! Highly recommended!!"
~ Fabrice Beliard, Australian Business Coach and Best Selling Author.

"A *Journey of Riches* Series is a must-read. It is an empowering collection of inspirational and moving stories full of courage, strength, and heart. Bringing peace and awareness to those lucky enough to read to assist and inspire them on their life journey."
~ Gemma Castiglia, Avalon Healing, Best Selling Author.

"The *A Journey of Riches* book series is an inspirational collection of books that will empower you to take on any challenge or change in life."
~ Kay Newton, Midlife Stress Buster, and Best Selling Author.

"A *Journey of Riches* book series is an inspiring collection of stories, sharing many different ideas and perspectives on how to overcome challenges, deal with change and to make empowering choices in your life. Open the book anywhere and let your mood choose where you need to read. Buy one of the books today; you'll be glad that you did!"
~ Trish Rock, Modern Day Intuitive, Bestselling Author, Speaker, Psychic & Holistic Coach.

"A *Journey of Riches* is another inspiring read. The authors are from all over the world, and each has a unique perspective to share, that will have you

thinking differently about your current circumstances in life. An insightful read!"
~ Alexandria Calamel, Success Coach and Best Selling Author.

"The A *Journey of Riches* book series is a collection of real-life stories, which are truly inspiring and give you the confidence that no matter what you are dealing with in your life, there is a light at the end of the tunnel, and a very bright one at that. Totally empowering!"
~ John Abbott, Freedom Entrepreneur.

"An amazing collection of true stories from individuals who have overcome great changes and who have transformed their lives and used their experience to uplift, inspire and support others."
~ Carol Williams, Author-Speaker-Coach.

"You can empower yourself from the power within this book that can help awaken the sleeping giant within you. John has a purpose in life to bring inspiring people together to share their wisdom for the benefit of all who venture deep into this book series. If you are looking for inspiration to be someone special, this book can be your guide."
~ Bill Bilwani, Renowned Melbourne Restaurateur.

"In the *A Journey Of Riches* series, you will catch the impulse to step up, reconsider and settle for only the very best for yourself and those around you. Penned from the heart and with an unflinching drive to make a difference for the good of all, *A Journey Of Riches* series is a must-read."
~ Steve Coleman, author of Decisions, Decisions! How to Make the Right One Every Time.

"Do you want to be on top of your game? *A Journey of Riches* is a must-read with breakthrough insights that will help you do just that!"
~ Christopher Chen, Entrepreneur.

"In *A Journey of Riches*, you will find the insight, resources, and tools you need to transform your life. By reading the author's stories, you, too, can be inspired to achieve your greatest accomplishments and what is truly possible for you. Reading this book activates your true potential for transforming your life way beyond what you think is possible. Read it and learn how you, too, can have a magical life."
~ Elaine Mc Guinness, Bestselling Author of Unleash Your Authentic Self!

"If you are looking for an inspiring read, look no further than the *A Journey Of Riches* book series. The books are an inspiring collection of short stories that

will encourage you to embrace life even more. I highly recommend you read one of the books today!"
~ Kara Dono, Doula, Healer and Best Selling Author.

"*A Journey of Riches* series is a must-read for anyone seeking to enrich their own lives and gain wisdom through the wonderful stories of personal empowerment & triumphs over life's challenges. I've given several copies to my family, friends, and clients to inspire and support them to step into their greatness. I highly recommend that you read these books, savoring the many 'aha's' and tools you will discover inside."
~ Michele Cempaka, Hypnotherapist, Shaman, Transformational Coach & Reiki Master.

"If you are looking for an inspirational read, look no further than the A *Journey Of Riches* book series. The books are an inspiring and educational collection of short stories from the author's soul that will encourage you to embrace life even more. I've even given them to my clients too so that their journeys inspire them in life for wealth, health and everything else in between. I recommend you make it a priority to read one of the books today!"
~ Goro Gupta, Chief Education Officer, Mortgage Terminator, Property Mentor.

"The A *Journey Of Riches* book series is filled with real-life short stories of heartfelt tribulations turned into uplifting, self-transformation by the power of the human spirit to overcome adversity. The journeys captured in these books will encourage you to embrace life in a whole new way. I highly recommend reading this inspiring anthology series."
~ Chris Drabenstott, Best Selling Author, and Editor.

"There is so much motivational power in the A *Journey of Riches* series!! Each book is a compilation of inspiring, real-life stories by several different authors, which makes the journey feel more relatable and success more attainable. If you are looking for something to move you forward, you'll find it in one (or all) of these books."
~ Cary MacArthur, Personal Empowerment Coach

"I've been fortunate to write with John Spender and now, I call him a friend. A *Journey of Riches* book series features real stories that have inspired me and will inspire you. John has a passion for finding amazing people from all over the world, giving the series a global perspective on relevant subject matters."
~ Mike Campbell, Fat Guy Diary, LLC

"The *A Journey of Riches* series is the reflection of beautiful souls who have discovered the fire within. Each story takes you inside the truth of what truly matters in life. While reading these stories, my heart space expanded to understand that our most significant contribution in this lifetime is to give and receive love. May you also feel inspired as you read this book."

~ Katie Neubaum, Author of Transformation Calling.

"*A Journey of Riches* is an inspiring testament that love and gratitude are the secret ingredients to living a happy and fulfilling life. This series is sure to inspire and bless your life in a big way. Truly an inspirational read that is written and created by real people, sharing real-life stories about the power and courage of the human spirit."

~ Jen Valadez, Emotional Intuitive and Best Selling Author

Table of Contents

CHAPTER SEVEN

CHAPTER EIGHT

CHAPTER NINE

CHAPTER TEN

---- ❖ ----

Preface

I collated this book and chose this collection of authors to share their experience about how they view love and what it means to return to love. This is to assist you raise your belief that you too deserve love. Just by being a living breathing human being you are worthy of love.

Like all of us, each author has a unique story and insight to share with you. It just might be the case that one or more of these authors have lived through an experience that is similar to circumstances in your life right now. Their words could be just the words you need to read to help you through your challenges and motivate you to continue on your journey.

Storytelling has been the way humankind has communicated ideas and learning throughout our civilization. While we have become more sophisticated with technology, and living in the modern world is more convenient, there is still much discontent and dissatisfaction. Many people have also moved away from reading books, and they are missing valuable information that can help them to move forward in life with a positive outlook.

I think it is essential to turn off the T.V.; to slow down and to read, reflect, and take the time to appreciate everything you have in life.

I like anthology books because they illustrate many different perspectives and insights on a singular topic. I find that sometimes when I'm reading books with just one author, I gain an understanding of their viewpoint and writing style very quickly, and the reading becomes predictable. With this book, and all of the books in the A Journey of Riches book series, you have many different writing styles and viewpoints that will help shape your perspective towards your current set of circumstances.

Anthology books are also great because you can start from any chapter and gain valuable insight or a nugget of wisdom without the feeling that you have missed something from the earlier episodes.

I love reading many different types of personal development books because learning and personal growth is vital to me. If you are not learning and growing, well, you're staying the same. Everything in the universe is growing, expanding, and changing. If we are not open to different ideas and different ways of thinking and being, then we can become close-minded.

The concept of this book series is to open you up to different ways of perceiving your reality. It is to encourage you and give you many avenues of thinking about the same subject. My wish for you is to feel empowered to make a decision that will best suit you in moving forward with your life. As Albert Einstein said, "We cannot solve problems with the same level of thinking that created them."

With Einstein's words in mind, let your mood pick a chapter in the book, or read from the beginning to the end and allow yourself to be guided to find the answers you seek.

If you feel inspired, we would love an honest review on Amazon.

With gratitude,
John Spender

"If we dive deep enough into ourselves,
we will find the one thread of universal
love that ties all beings together."

~ Amma

CHAPTER ONE

❖

The Moment Being A "Bad Boy" Changed My World

By Robin Seeger

Every moment in time, I have a choice. This chapter is about one of these moments and the ripple effects my awareness in this one situation would have for many future events and decisions. The key to this transformation was in discovering this awareness and healing from the trauma that had influenced my earlier life.

I was picking up Raphael, my 10-year-old son, from school, and we were on our way home when we came to the main intersection in Ubud, Bali. As do most drivers on their motorbikes, we would make our way past the cars waiting at the red light to go to the front. Often, when no car or motorcycle is in sight, people take a left-hand turn even when the light is on red.

I chose to do the same that afternoon. As soon as I took off, I saw the policeman jumping out behind a wall yelling at me. I knew right away I'd gotten caught. "Stop, Stop, Stop," he shouted. And then I heard his loud whistle several times. I looked him in the eye and told him I would pull over. My son whispered from behind me, "Daddy, I think you are in trouble." This was when my heart and chest contracted and my mind went into overdrive. I had about thirty to forty seconds to cross the road and talk to the policeman, who glared at me.

What am I going to say? I felt anger rising. He would not have stopped a Balinese driver. He just wants to get some money. This is so unfair! These were just a few of the many thoughts that were racing through my mind.

When I stood in front of him, he asked me in his broken English if I knew why he'd stopped me. I felt like saying, "No I don't. I didn't do anything wrong. Why did you stop me but not the Balinese driver that did the same just 30 seconds earlier?" But I did not. I had a moment of awareness. None of this felt right; I have learned to listen to my body, and when I feel any contraction or tightness, these are signs that something is not right.

This is not who I am anymore, I thought. This was old programming that sometimes still tries to come back into my consciousness. This was how I would have reacted five or ten years ago. So, instead of being defensive, my response to the officer was: "Yes, Sir, I crossed the line while the light was still red and was making a left turn illegally. I take full responsibility. I am very sorry. I know I made a mistake."

This definitely caught the police officer off guard, and he paused for a moment instead of lecturing me or continuing to interrogate me. He simply asked me for my driver's license and my registration. I handed him both, and he went to a makeshift table where he would usually write out a ticket for the traffic violation.

He sat down, pretending to check my papers, but he didn't even look at the right page. He took a long time to formulate his response. When he came back, he asked me, "So you know you did something wrong?"

"Yes." I replied once more without thinking. "Yes, I did something wrong; I drove through a red light and I am very sorry." He looked at my son and me and digested that answer once more. His demeanor shifted completely.

There is more to this story, and I will get back to it in a moment. But what does this story have to do with returning to love? Why is this so important?

Because, as I mentioned, not too long ago I would have reacted very differently. I would have felt mistreated. I would have had a passive-aggressive response because I would have thought that I needed to defend myself in this or any similar situation.

I have had my fair share of run-ins with authorities in which I felt I was being wronged, and I often saw authority as the image of that tall, big, white, bald intimidating looking guy.

When I was in my 20s and 30s, every time I was traveling at the airport, I would get chosen from the security line for a "random" special screening. At a border crossing, my car would be "randomly" selected for a secondary inspection. When going to a concert or a sports event, I would have to have a "random" pat down.

I would always blame it on others, on the system being wrong, on me being a perceived "bad boy" just because of my looks, or on somebody having a bad day and choosing me as a target to let out their frustrations. I often made up excuses for their behavior in my head: how maybe their partner just broke up with them, how they must have gotten up on the wrong side of the bed in the morning, or how something else bad must have happened to them.

Not once did I consider the possibility of this being because of me—not that I actually was a bad person, but that might have been how I came across when somebody encountered me for the first time in these kinds of situations. I could be intimidating; I would rebel by challenging the randomness of these treatments while raising my voice, by standing up tall.

Honestly, looking back at all of these moments in time, they were often embarrassing, and the worst was I didn't see anything wrong with my responses. Yes, I would feel embarrassed afterward and I didn't feel good about how I'd acted, but it was such a natural response that I did not feel the need to change anything. As I said before, it wasn't my fault anyway.

Until something very magical happened. I became a dad for the first time in my mid-thirties. First, my son was born and, a few years later, my daughter was born. Within the first few years, I started to realize something had to change. My children were way-showers, true and natural guides in my life. They made me understand that there is so much more to this issue. Through them entering into my life, I discovered it was not about my rebel soul trying to challenge authorities; it was about a little boy inside of me crying out for attention. This little boy felt like he was being mistreated and had been for most of his life. This child had felt judged, bullied, and ridiculed and told what to do by his friends, his teachers, his family...really all his surroundings.

This pattern started at an early age and continued through my teen years until I began to go through some growth spurts and became taller and stronger on the outside. I would grow taller than even the older bullies and would learn to use that height. It took me until just a few years ago to truly realize that the growth on the outside did not match the growth on the inside. It was just a mask; this was a pretend me that was strong, not to be messed with, and I was done with being bullied. In reality, I was still the same on the inside, an insecure little boy that felt unlovable, not good enough, not seen or heard, and always living in defense mode trying to not get hurt, trying to avoid being bullied or treated unfairly again.

Over time, this led me to move from living from my heart space to living more from my headspace. This would reflect in many aspects of my life, but I was mostly aware of it when I entered into a relationship with a woman. I tried to look all confident. But deep inside of me, I was still afraid of being hurt, and so I would silently and unknowingly sabotage the relationship. I would always be worried that I would lose my girlfriend to a better guy. I was afraid that envious people were right when they told me that our relationship wouldn't last, that I was just a rebound or simply not good enough.

Looking back at my relationships, I realized that these kinds of thoughts were always in the back of my mind. They were the ones that drove me into changing who I really was. I would turn into someone different. I would try to be the person I thought someone wanted me to be, to be more desirable rather than understanding that I was loved for who I was.

This would be the case in many areas of my life; no matter my achievements, I would rarely acknowledge them as being enough, as there was just no capacity to truly love myself.

No matter how many people tried to tell me, I could never hear them. One day, my wife told me that I have a frozen heart, that although I'd found a way to protect myself from being hurt, I was also depriving myself of genuinely feeling anything. I did not hear it. How could that be true when I loved her so deeply? And how could she fall in love with me if she knew that to be true?

Then my children came along, and they did something nobody else was able to do. They mirrored my behavior, showed me the raw, authentic me that was on the inside without holding back, and they did so in a way that I could not ignore any longer.

Now, you have to understand that this didn't happen overnight; it took years and a radical change in our lifestyle as a family. During the first few years of my son's life, I was working first in a job that had me away from home for most of the day, and I traveled extensively. When I realized that this wasn't working for us, I thought about taking a job that would be closer to home and without travel, hoping that would make a difference. It didn't, as I still left the house before my kids woke up and wouldn't come home until they were ready to go to bed.

At this point, we decided as a family to leave that lifestyle behind and start over. We saw how our family was falling apart and how we were getting more and more disconnected, although our life looked amazing on the outside.

Within six months of making this decision, we sold all of our possessions and began our travel adventure. We had four suitcases and a romantic thought of connecting again as a family while showing our children that there are other lifestyles and different ways of living than what they had experienced so far.

First, we flew to Japan, then to Singapore, then to Indonesia, and then later to New Zealand, to Fiji, and to Australia. We traveled for about 15 months and during this time spent nearly all day and night together as a family.

This is when the change started happening. Being able to witness my son's behavior on a daily basis allowed me to create awareness around my own behavior. I started seeing my own inner child in him. Right in front of my eyes, my son was developing a true reflection of who I was as a kid growing up.

First, I didn't want to acknowledge it—it was too painful, too deeply hidden in my subconscious—but over time I had no choice. If I didn't want my son to live my life over, and if I wanted to allow him to grow fully into his own identity, then I would have to start looking inside myself and learn to heal old wounds so that the interior could begin to match the exterior. I needed to become the man I really was, which meant dismantling the façade, ripping off that mask that kept me feeling safe for so long. I needed to face my emotional self; I needed to learn to listen to what felt right to my heart and soul rather than listening to a construct created by my mind so I wouldn't get hurt anymore.

I often asked myself why I didn't see this earlier. Well, it was because the construct didn't work. I still got hurt. My heart got ripped into pieces many times. And every time I thought I was being my true self and I got hurt, I believed it was because somebody else did something wrong. I just couldn't see that it was because of that little boy inside of me who was running the show, running my life from a place of deep hurt and not feeling safe in this world.

How did this awareness come to me? Through daily observation and by slowly connecting the dots. As I had the opportunity to witness my children day and night, I started to see their true natures. I began to distinguish the different emotional states they were in and where they were coming from, but then there were also moments where nothing made sense. First, I thought this was related to them being children, but then I started to connect my own mental and emotional state to theirs. I realized how my being stressed, angry, frustrated, sad, tired, or my being happy, relaxed, or energetic would have a direct impact on their behavior.

I couldn't blame too much sugar, not enough sleep, bad influences from other kids, or even the fact that they are just children. It just couldn't be a coincidence that, every time I was going through an emotional shift in my being, they would shift as well. So, one day when they were running rampant, one tantrum after the other, and not listening to a word I was saying, I stopped. I took a deep breath, removed myself from the situation, and asked myself what was going on inside of me. I was stressed, overwhelmed, and short in my responses, but that wasn't it. This did not feel like the reason for their behavioral change. I had to dig deeper, and at that moment, I looked at my son and saw myself—my young self trying to get the attention of my parents. When I was growing up, I was to be seen but not heard, so I got attention by acting out.

Not having enough space to meet their growing needs at the time created reactions. Later, when I asked them if they remembered what happened to them, why they acted the way they did, my son and my daughter did not have an explanation. They simply looked at me and said, "Daddy, I don't know." This was the next clue in a series of many. They did not act this way for a specific reason; they acted like this as a direct result of my energies being projected onto them. They couldn't explain it; they didn't care. Even worse, they saw it as normal.

For me, this was far from normal. It was a revelation of such magnitude that I had to do something. I could not allow my children to be unable to deal with their emotions because of me. I wanted them to experience all of their feelings. I wanted them to go wild because they wanted to explore their boundaries and their limitations, not because I was overwhelmed or stressed. I wanted them to feel what it means to be sad when something heartbreaking happens to them and to know I would be there when they needed me, fully present to support and guide them through any experience. I wanted them to have healthy experiences with anger and frustration or any other emotion. And the only way that I could make this possible was to allow myself to feel, to come to a place of love for myself.

From that moment on, I would allow myself to look at all of these little boys inside of me. There was one for every year of my life. I would start to connect with this inner child, and, through this connection, I could get in touch with my emotions. Over time, the relationship would become more; it would evolve into a dialog with myself. First, it would be simple: "How are you?

What do you need today?" Then we went deeper: "When was the first time you felt unlovable? When did you feel like you weren't heard? How did it feel to be bullied? What was going on inside of you when you were told boys don't cry or don't know pain?"

The more space I created for these conversations, the more detailed the answers became. Often the responses came in the form of forgotten or suppressed memories. One time in one of the parenting workshops I facilitated, during an inner child meditation, the question of not being heard was asked. And at that moment, I remembered how my "friends" would have me hogtied to a wall in my parent's garage. I would try to make myself noticeable, but for what felt like an eternity, nobody would come. I had tears rolling down my cheeks; I had buried the feeling of this situation for decades.

I had to dig deep and reparent myself. I had to teach myself what is and what is not okay in my life in this moment. I needed to learn to create healthy boundaries; I needed to understand that it is okay not to be okay. To enable my children to connect with their emotions, I needed to leave my comfort zone and become this authentic version of myself whom I could love unconditionally at any time.

This included me falling apart one day while having breakfast with my whole family in a hip restaurant. I was overcome with sadness, and tears started rolling down my cheek. My first thought was, "Not now, not here. What will all these people think?" This was quickly followed by, "What will my kids think?" This is when I really started sobbing, when that little boy just wanted to cry, to not have to hold back his tears any longer.

So, I did cry, and both of my children came and sat next to me. "Are you okay, Daddy?" they said simultaneously. "Yes, I am; I just have this huge feeling of sadness in me and I need a moment to feel it." My family sat with me for a few minutes while I allowed myself to feel every little thing that was alive. Like a friend of mine always says, "Feeling is healing." I was healing years and years of suppressed feelings at this moment and, at the same time, my children became empowered to do the same. They were okay with me not being okay at that moment, and they subsequently knew it is okay for them not to be okay and that they could let out their emotions with me by their sides whenever they need to do so and would feel safe.

This change in me created a huge shift in the story this chapter opened with. As mentioned, the policeman's behavior shifted. He stopped talking about what I did wrong. Then his face softened and, in broken English, he started nearly apologetically explaining why he had stopped us. "I just stopped you to keep you safe," he explained. I did not see that coming. "There are many drivers that don't pay attention, and what if you would have gotten into an accident?"

He returned my papers to me and, without a ticket, sent us on our way. "I hope you and your son have a beautiful day. And please stay safe. Hati Hati." (Indonesian meaning to be cautious.) I didn't know what to do; I was expecting a ticket and a lecture. I expected to have to explain to my son that even though everybody else does something wrong, it is still against the law and the officer had the right to fine us. Instead, I took my license and insurance papers and followed my son back to our motorbike. The moment we got back on the bike and continued our drive home, my son tapped me on the shoulder and said, "Daddy you just got stopped by the police for doing something wrong and got away with it." And then he added with the biggest smirk, "You were a bad boy."

Now I am not endorsing or trying to justify in any way what I did that day, but I am seeing how the love I'd found for myself and how choosing a path of living authentically had helped me to empower the policeman to look at his choices, as well as allowing my son to realize that owning up to our mistakes and speaking the truth does not necessarily result in punishment.

In that moment, I was for the first time in my life proud to be a Bad Boy, and I loved that boy more than ever.

"If love is universal no one can be left out."

~ Deepak Chopra

CHAPTER TWO

❖

Healing the Family Soul

By Julie Williams

"Where there is love, there is life."
~ Mahatma Gandhi

What if I told you there was one key thing you could do to align your mind, body, and spirit with truth, love, and happiness? This thing could assist you in shifting the foundation of who you are so deeply and profoundly that you could stop seeking what you wanted and actually start living your dreams. You would be motivated by love rather than fear, allowing you to access a steady flow of self-empowerment that is aligned with your soul's true purpose.

Over the last two decades of facilitating thousands of clients, students, and retreat participants through Family Constellation Therapy, I've witnessed incredible results across all kinds of physical, emotional, and spiritual issues. For example, I've helped women who were told they were infertile to birth several healthy children. I've assisted people in healing completely from conditions like depression, chronic fatigue, panic attacks, cancer, and many others. I've seen relationships on the brink of disaster find love and connection again. I've assisted people in turning their businesses around from bankruptcy to profitability. Time and time again, I've seen the power of Family Constellation Therapy change people's lives in ways that align them with manifesting what their hearts desire most, while simultaneously releasing them from the burdens of suffering they have unknowingly inherited from their ancestors.

Family Constellation Therapy is a systemic approach which uncovers and releases unconscious entanglements to ancestral suffering that affect our health and well-being both personally and professionally. It is based on the idea that just as we have our own soul or animating life force energy, our family has collective energy called the family soul. The family soul holds life and is bound by deep, all-encompassing and unwavering love.

As life flows from generation to generation, the family soul weaves a beautiful tapestry giving each family member a place within the masterpiece. Like your fingerprint, your place within the family soul belongs only to you. When all family members take their place within the system, there is a natural order that presides, allowing love to be the primary force that flows in life. However, if anyone in your family history experienced trauma, loss of a child, mental illness, an early death, imprisonment, or any ill fate that meant they were excluded, lost, forgotten, or estranged, the family soul becomes fragmented and the flow of love is disrupted. Like water that leaks from a cracked vase, the family soul cannot hold its full life force if any family members are forgotten. This means that the future generations will only have a fraction of the life force available to them, which will inevitably lead to some form of pain, suffering, or distress in life.

Take a moment to think about the lives of your parents, grandparents, or great-grandparents. I'm willing to bet you'll be able to identify someone in your family history who experienced something that had an impact on your family soul. If you compare their experience to a current struggle in your own life, you'll probably notice a striking similarity. This is an example of an entanglement. Some of the strongest entanglements can also be found where the family history is unknown or missing. Given world history, it's safe to say we all have something in our ancestral past that has impacted our family soul enough to create entanglements that cause suffering in our lives today. Here's why:

In addition to inheriting our genetic information from our ancestors, we also line up to take on the burdens of suffering, especially the ones that caused a family member to be excluded and the family soul to fracture. By living the same suffering now, our hope is that we can heal the wound to the family soul, by re-including them through living a similar experience. We do this out of deep love and loyalty as our souls try to honor their lives by trying to feel their pain. In other words, in an effort to heal the wounds of the past, we take them on as our own. These are deep subconscious patterns that we are rarely aware of until they begin to have a negative impact on our life. When we can understand that our pain will not heal the pain for another, but instead, only create more pain, then we have taken the first step in breaking free from our ancestral entanglements.

While love and loyalty are an important part of why we take on the family suffering, the most compelling reason is our need to belong to our family system. Think about a newborn baby for a moment. It's cute and smells nice but is completely helpless on its own. Every child needs someone to care for it in order to survive, which is how the need to belong becomes hardwired into our psyche as a primary instinct. To survive, we must first belong. This explains why we willingly take on our family pain. To separate from it pushing against our basic survival instincts. Essentially, we are deciding that it is better to suffer by living with ancestral entanglements than risk our survival by not belonging.

When we accept that our belonging in our family system is guaranteed by fully taking our appropriate place in our family system, we free ourselves from the hold the entanglements have on us. From this place, we can acknowledge all members of the family with full honor and respect, allowing in a deep knowing that everyone belongs, no matter what. This is a profoundly important part of how we can bring peace and healing to every member of every family, including ourselves, because when we heal ourselves, we heal the entire family bloodline.

The first time I heard this explanation of the principles behind the work from my Family Constellation therapist, Eve, I was a bit bewildered yet eager to learn more:

"You mean to tell me that I am suffering in my life as a form of misdirected love in an attempt to heal the past, which isn't possible, and also to try to belong, which is already a certainty?," I said, shaking my head in disbelief. "That doesn't seem like the best use of my time," I mused.

"Yes, that's exactly what you and all of us, are doing in the deepest recesses of our subconscious minds," Eve responded.

"OK, so I'm carrying burdens from the past but they don't belong to me at all?"

"Precisely. Because you love your family so deeply, you subconsciously agree to take on their suffering."

"Honestly, that seems a bit rude. I mean, it's like I'm expressing through my actions that they can't handle it or aren't strong enough to cope."

"Yes, I suppose it is a bit rude," she laughed.

I questioned, "If I suffer in my life now, which doesn't actually take away the suffering of my great-grandmother, then aren't I actually creating more of the pain in the family soul system as a whole?" A wave of sadness passed over me.

"Yes, you're exactly right," she replied gently. "Your soul's prayer goes something like this:

Dear great-grandmother, I will be the one who suffers in this lifetime so that you would never have had to suffer in your life. I do this because I love you and want to heal the wounds within our family system. I do this out of deep loyalty to our family soul, which guarantees my belonging and, therefore, allows me to stay safe and alive. My deepest desire is that if I can take on your suffering, then there is hope that all the generations who come after me can be free from similar trauma, illness, distress, unhappiness, hardship, and pain. I will give my life to this purpose because when those who came before me are healed, I will be healed too; then we may all (including my children) be able to embrace life more fully and live with a heart full of love, peace, and unity."

"Wow, that's strangely beautiful," I replied. "But wait...does that mean I'm completely screwed? I mean, I can't change what happened in the past, so am I forever sentenced to the pain?" I was starting to feel a bit trapped and hopeless, as if my free will had just been taken from me.

With a soft chuckle, she replied, "Not at all, quite the opposite, really. Coming to realize what your subconscious mind has been up to for so long is the first step to being able to change the pattern and let go of the burdens you carry in your life that don't belong to you. Family Constellation work is the most effective way I know of to release these ancestral entanglements so you can access the fullness of your life. When you reclaim the love you were putting into what you now realize is an impossible task, it comes back to you in such beautiful and magical ways. I, for one, am looking forward to seeing what you do with it in your life because I know it will be something special." She beamed a smile in my direction.

"I feel lighter already in just acknowledging that," I replied in relief. "And now I feel really drawn to setting up my own constellation to give back what isn't mine and create a life that's guided by love rather than fear. Is that a possibility?" I asked, wiping the remnant of a tear from my cheek.

She replied with a kindness that opened my heart just a little more than it was before. "Yes, I'd be honored to walk that path with you."

At that time, I was a senior executive working at a large biotech company based in San Francisco, California. I was at the peak of my corporate success, having worked my way up the corporate ladder from

my early days in the lab doing genetic research. I'd
worked hard, channeling my competitive spirit and
goal-oriented nature into my career, and it had paid
off. My lifestyle matched the big salary I was earning
with a shiny new car, regular travel on our corporate
jet, and a house I'd purchased completely on my own.
The drawback was that I was always striving for the
next goal, seldom taking time to rest, and I soon found
myself in a state of burnout. The hard work that was
necessary to create a successful career was now
beginning to stifle my personal happiness.

When a long-term relationship ended suddenly, and I
no longer had the energy to compete in the
endurance racing I'd enjoyed so much because it
helped me find perspective, my emotions began to
overwhelm me on a fairly regular basis. I was smart
enough to recognize something wasn't quite right, but
I couldn't put my finger on precisely what it was,
which is why I paid close attention to that chance
meeting that happened with Eve. She gave me an
important message at the exact time I was looking for
it.

I'd learned to trust these synchronicities in life, so I
began to reflect a little more on what made me happy
in life and what didn't. I noticed how little happiness I

actually felt working in my current career, even though I was good at it. When I searched for where my passion for work was, I realized I was much happier working with clients as a holistic therapist, which I was doing on the side as time allowed. It caused me to remember my childhood desire to become a doctor because I wanted to help people heal. I originally got my degree in Biology with the intention of applying to medical school but later changed my mind when I found I just couldn't stand behind the traditional medical model of diagnosis and pharmaceutical treatments. It seemed more limited than what I knew true healing to be. Going into research was the next best option for me, where I could focus on healing people by providing scientific knowledge to the world.

I began to wonder, if I wasn't happy in my work, then why was I so driven to succeed in it? If my passion lies elsewhere, then what was fueling me to stay in my current career? The simple answer was fear — fear of not having enough and not being good enough. I soon found myself back in conversation with Eve. I explained my realization and wondered if she could shed some light on it from the ancestral perspective.

"I think my success is driven by fear," I admitted on a warm summer day, as we sat looking out the window together, drinking a cup of tea.

"Fear is an extremely powerful motivator," she nodded. "But the problem with that strategy is that it's not sustainable in the long term; it will catch up with you eventually."

I nodded in agreement. "Yeah, I think I'm at that point. I'm pretty burned out," I admitted with a sigh. I felt like everything in my life was unraveling, crashing down, and exploding all at the same time. I had lost the connection to my inner knowing that had previously brought clarity for what my next steps should be. No matter what I did, I couldn't shake the growing fear of failure that threatened to drown me.

"That's good that you can acknowledge that," she said encouragingly. "You have to be able to admit there's an issue before you can begin to heal it. Are there other areas of your life where you feel fear is a bigger player in your decisions that you might like it to be?" she continued. "You can tell there is an ancestral component to the stress if the same experience or emotion shows up in multiple contexts in your life."

"Yes, actually, I can see how the same fear plays out in my romantic relationships, too."

"How so?" she asked, turning toward me to listen more carefully.

"Well, my current pattern in relationships is that I choose unavailable men. It never works out, for obvious reasons, and it always makes me feel afraid that I'm not good enough or loveable. Or, if they want to commit to me, I can't reciprocate the commitment because I'm afraid they won't be enough for me in the long term," I explained.

"It sounds like you've done work in this area before. That's a pretty self-realized statement," she said thoughtfully.

"Yes, I've been doing some personal growth work around this, but it doesn't seem to move me forward. I'm still a magnet for the same type of guy, which is pretty frustrating, but I can't seem to break free from it," I shared. My last breakup sent me into the tailspin of questioning every aspect of my life. I figured if I could release the suffering underneath my failed relationships, maybe this would help me in the other areas of my life as well.

Eve explained, "That's exactly how it feels when there are ancestral entanglements at play. You can't seem to break free from the situation because the deep loyalties and survival instinct to belong are attached to staying loyal to the suffering. I think it would help you if we set up a constellation on it. Would that be of interest to you?"

My curiosity was beginning to peak and I was excited to explore what might be at the root of my struggles. "Yes, I'd be open to that," I replied. As I began to understand the concept better, I was curious to know how far-reaching one piece of work could be. I asked, "Will working with the context of relationships also help my career issue as well? Or is that a separate constellation?"

"Good question," she said. "When we uncover and release the ancestral entanglements you carry in the context of relationships, it will also have a positive effect on releasing the same pattern for you in your career. I call this the holistic nature of the work; working each part affects the whole. Shall we schedule a constellation for you at my next group workshop?"

"Yes, I'd love that, thank you," I replied. I was excited but apprehensive since I really didn't have any idea what was in store for me. Could this work be the key to unlocking a happier future for me? Could it free me from the fear that had been motivating me? Would it be powerful enough to unravel decades of conditioning that I'd been living with and help me find true love? It would take some time, but I would find that the answer to all these questions was a resounding yes.

We met again the following weekend at a group Family Constellation workshop she was hosting. Having my own constellation done was exciting, terrifying, and surreal all at the same time. I remember being instantly fascinated by the process, but also feeling, extremely vulnerable about baring my soul to a room full of strangers who had gathered that day to participate.

From our previous conversations, we agreed the issue we would work with was to explore what was stopping me from finding a healthy, long-term relationship. With the issue clear at hand, Eve skillfully collected my family history, then chose participants from the group to be representatives for my family members. These representatives were placed within the circle of chairs where everyone was seated and asked to stand in the field and report on their experiences. What unfolded on the floor in front of me was something I'd never seen before.

The representatives were clearly themselves, yet also were expressing emotions, thoughts, and mannerisms in an uncanny way, capturing my family dynamic so precisely; I was astounded. How did they know that was how my mother held herself or how my father spoke or what their relationship dynamic was? How did my representative know where to stand concerning my parents, reflecting the truth of my part in the whole dynamic?

I watched in awe as Eve used words, movements, and positioning to draw out the hidden suffering in my family system, which allowed me to take my appropriate place in the structure, all the while, including everyone who was excluded with full honor and respect. As I sat there in a room full of people who were playing out my family dynamic before me with such devotion, unconditional love, and support, I knew at that moment that Family Constellation work was something truly extraordinary.

What transpired next was pure magic and brought the clarity I was seeking. As my constellation unfolded before me, I sat in disbelief as I witnessed what we discovered next. Two representatives laid on the floor

— one representing me and the other for the 'thing' that kept me from finding my beloved. They faced each other, completely mirroring the other's position, gestures, and expressions. (Representatives that lie on the floor are symbolic of not being alive or not accepting life.) As these two people laid at the feet of the representatives of my parents, Eve looked at me with a knowing gaze. She'd seen this dynamic many times in her career and named it the "womb twin dynamic."

Womb twins are sole survivors of a twin or multiple pregnancy. Most commonly, the lost twin is miscarried within the first trimester without the mother's knowledge. As soon as the words were spoken in the field, the representative for my mother collapsed, sobbing next to the lost twin, while the representative for my father stood stunned and disconnected. As I sat there, taking it all in, I began to feel seen in a way I had never been before.

I watched as Eve worked tenderly, straightforwardly, and adeptly to re-include this lost one so that both of my parents' souls could finally acknowledge their loss. I felt a tremendous burden lift from my heart. What remained was a sense of wholeness — a knowing that I am indeed enough within myself. At that moment, every failed relationship I'd ever had suddenly made sense. The great loves in my life had been my manifestation of my lost twin, not my soulmate. The fear of being born without my twin had driven me to try to fill the empty place with material possessions, career successes, and monetary rewards. I had been waiting to find my other half before I would allow myself to fully live.

This was a game-changer for me. A whole new identity aligned with my soul's truth was now available and I didn't have to do anything but simply be me. The gift this piece of work gave me that day would transform my life forever.

Almost instantly, my life began to change. Straight away, I noticed my ability to stay calm in situations that used to cause me anxiety. The kind of men I attracted and chose to be in a relationship with were more available and I was able to commit deeply to them. I felt more solid and grounded as I accessed a deeper embodiment of my own essence. My self-confidence was restored, and I could fully trust my inner guidance once more. The noise in my head, otherwise known as the monkey mind, fell silent. I was able to fully relax and recover from my burnout without feeling guilty or lazy. My future felt full of potential and my path began to unfold before me.

My life circumstances soon changed to catch up with the inner soul transformation I'd experienced. I was able to negotiate a deal to leave my corporate job with eight months full salary in my pocket as a thank you for my many years of dedicated service and hard work. I felt so supported by my ancestors to grant me the gift of time without having to worry about money. My wish for a career change came true, and I was able to step full-time into being a holistic therapist and facilitator. Lastly, all my relationships were doing better than ever.

In a follow-up conversation after my own constellation, I sat with Eve by the fire, sharing reflections on what had transpired. As I explored the work more deeply, I discovered that there are a few main movements associated with healing the family soul. She described them as the "big/little dynamic," "interrupted reaching out," the "victim/perpetrator," and "life's embrace." I asked her which movements we had done in my constellation the previous day. I was eager to find out if I could do more work since I'd found the first session so valuable.

Eve explained, "Mostly, I worked with the big/little dynamic because it was your first constellation and that is the foundational movement. The parents are the big ones and the children are the little ones — it's the order we arrive on the planet. It isn't appropriate for the little ones to take responsibility for the big ones and the suffering their souls may carry."

"That makes sense; it would be rude to do that," I mused, remembering our first conversation. "I can see why it's a foundational movement; it had an incredibly powerful effect on me."

"I'm glad you got to benefit from it,' she replied. "Your system was really ready to make the move, which always helps bring change more quickly without a whole lot of drama."

"Yeah, the only drama I have now is in trying to get enough clients so my business can support me financially," I said. "I still have to dip into my savings for unexpected expenses. There seems to be an invisible limit to what I can earn in business for myself rather than when I'm working for someone else."

"That's interesting. Did anyone in your ancestral past lose a business, get swindled out of a family fortune, get cut out of a will, or lose the family home?"

I went on to tell Eve the story of my grandfather, who was orphaned at a young age, and by the time he was old enough to claim the family fortune, the lawyer managing the estate had spent every last cent, leaving him with nothing. His mother — my great-grandmother — made her fortune in real estate, only to lose it all in a shady investment deal. My father and his sister had a falling out after she took his share of their mother's inheritance, leaving him with nothing of the family estate.

"Those are indeed significant events that would cause you to become entangled in financial misfortune," Eve explained. "I sense that you have turned that loyalty around a bit, though, where, instead of losing the fortune, you won't allow yourself to receive it in the first place. After all, you can't lose what you don't have."

I was speechless. She'd hit the nail on the head. As she spoke, she had taken out a small wooden board and set small figurines on it representing each family member I had mentioned. This was a one-to-one format of doing constellations when you didn't have a group of people handy to set one up. I sat there captivated as she worked to release the ancestral entanglements I had around money.

"I like the balance I now feel in your masculine line," she commented, "and now my attention is going to your maternal line. Given that your mother lost a child, experienced trauma in her own childhood, and then lost her mother at a young age, interrupted reaching out is going to be present for you. This will hinder your ability to receive any form of abundance."

"Can you explain a little more about that?" I asked. She really had my attention now. What she said made perfect sense, and I could also feel it in my body. My heart ached, and tears began to fill my eyes. She noticed me trying to hold back the floodgates of my building emotions.

"It's ok," she said. "Let the emotions flow; grief is one of the heart's emotions, and when it heals, sometimes tears are needed to let go and open your heart to love completely. Keep the breath flowing; it helps to move the emotion."

She worked with the figurines on the board as she explained that interrupted reaching out is a soul movement (not a physical one) between mother and child after birth. When the child is separate from the mother's body, its soul reaches for the embrace of the mother. When this soul reach is met, the child's soul may then connect to life with the eternal love and support of their mother; however, if there is not enough of the mother's soul present to meet the reach of the child (due to her entanglements, lost children, or past trauma), the embrace is never realized, and the child stops reaching (thus the name).

My emotions went from a cathartic expression of grief to a tender vulnerability as she worked this dynamic using the board and figurines. I began to feel the heart-to-heart connection with my mother's soul as I was held in her soul's embrace. I longed for nothing in this place. I suddenly felt like I had everything I needed.

"I think that's a good place to leave it for today," Eve said, seeing the flush in my cheeks and fullness of my heart.

"There's one more movement I'd like to do with you after this piece integrates fully." I nodded in reply with deep gratitude for this work, her kindness, and skill.

Healing the interrupted reaching out pattern opened the doors to my business BIG TIME. My phone started ringing off the hook with clients wanting to work with me; I was being invited to give workshops, talks, and asked for interviews by newspapers, radio, and podcasts. The word about my holistic therapy business was now out there and I no longer had any problems filling my appointment book and workshops.

For the first time in my life, I was truly happy in my skin. I was working my passion, financially independent, and felt as ready as ever to settle down with someone and create a life together. That's when I met the man who I instantly recognized as a soulmate, and it was the icing on the cake! Looking back, I can see it was all a divinely orchestrated setup to bring me face to face with one of the darkest movements of the family soul, the victim-perpetrator pattern. It was a pattern I'd been acutely aware of in other contexts of my life over the years but couldn't release it thoroughly until it was a matter of true love.

The victim-perpetrator dynamic is one of the most common ancestral dynamics. It has to do with the events of the past where anyone was victimized or perpetrated a crime. We all have this energy somewhere in our past; it can show up as bullying, anger issues, abuse, victim mentality, bipolar disorder, autoimmune disorders, depression, anxiety, or other chronic illnesses.

Months later, I found myself back in the client chair for my next constellation session with Eve. I'd been sharing my successes with work and also my dismay in thinking I'd found "the one," but was now caught up in a web of lies, betrayal, and deceit. In my mind, the relationship was pretty stable until one day, everything changed when I found out what my partner had been up to behind my back. I was angry with myself for not seeing it sooner, saddened by what he'd done, and afraid of what he might do next.

"Fear, anger, and grief are the emotions associated with the victim/perpetrator dynamic," Eve pointed out to me. "Given your parents' ancestral makeup of Polish and German heritage, I'm not surprised you've got this running through you. The Holocaust is one example of a collective expression of this pattern. We'll need to work with this before we can do the last movement I had in mind."

Facilitating this pattern in the family constellation frame takes skill and experience, given the density associated with it. The key to healing it is to realize that all of these aspects are the same, meaning you can never have one without the other. Once these are united in harmony, the dynamic loses its hold on the lives of those who are caught up in it.

I watched her work with the victim/perpetrator dynamic by standing in to represent each aspect herself, which is another way a facilitator can work in a one-to-one session. She stepped back and forth between the two aspects, reporting what she noticed and working with the feelings that came up for me. She adeptly worked until no animosity or tension remained between the two aspects and a complete sense of God-like love and unity filled the room.

"Now it's time for you to feel life's embrace" she said, standing in front of me, representing life. I stood in as myself. We stood facing each other, arms outstretched but not touching.

"I want you to really reach for me, your life. Reach with an open heart. I am a representative of all the aspects of your life. See me as the pure life force energy that I am. I am pure love, limitless joy, and divine harmony. I am all you seek, and my purpose is to be what you make of me. I am you. You are me. We are one."

With those words, I felt as if I'd been pushed forward, although no one was behind me, and I flew into the arms of life. The embrace was indescribable. I was so full of light that my worries, discomforts, and distresses faded to the furthest edges of my awareness. I discovered at that moment that the best and most fulfilling way to be free from pain and suffering was to fill myself with the unconditional love of life force energy. Some might call this a moment of enlightenment or liberation. Once you experience it, you can never "unfeel" it. It changes who you are forever.

Life force energy is the most abundant kind of energy there is in the universe. It holds the fullness of every living being, while at the same time, is nothing but infinite potential until it is connected to a living soul who embodies it as their own. To access the fullness of life, we must free ourselves from the loyalties to our ancestral entanglements.

Family Constellation work is the most effective form of therapy I've come across that can do this in such a complete and lasting way. When you are free from these entanglements, the flow of love is restored so that you can welcome in all the abundance that life has to offer. For me, once I embraced life fully, the fear that had once been a constant companion no longer had power over me.

Instead of looking for love, I had finally become love. It was then that I was finally able to meet my beloved and discovered it was someone I'd known all along. I fell in love instantly.

My beloved was me. Falling completely in love with yourself is the place where true empowerment lies. My heartfelt wish for you is that you may realize that this love is not to be sought; it's within you…where it has been all along.

"We are all born for love.

It is the principal of

existence, and it's only end."

~ Benjamin Disraeli

CHAPTER THREE

※

Coming Home

By John Spender

In 2010 I was sitting with thousands of people at the Sydney Convention Centre in Darling Harbour. I felt a surge of energy flood into my heart when I heard Deepak Chopra say, "There are only two emotions: love and fear. Positive emotions come from love, all negative emotions from fear."

I had to stop and ponder: could our emotions boil down to two choices? Meaning, all the other emotions can be labeled either fear or love? If you are not expressing from a place of love you are coming from fear; that's an interesting concept to dive into and explore. I often think to myself, "Where does a particular fear derive from?" Usually, I trace it back to the fear of not feeling loved. My innate knowing about love is that it's universal, unconditional. Anyone can tap into it. I'm not really talking about emotional love, the kind that you can fall out of so quickly; emotional love feels material to me. Yes, it is important to have your emotional needs met. I'm talking about something more expansive. It's universal love -- universal love fills me with a sense of oneness, where anything is limitless. Before I get too airy-fairy with you, let me add that I think society's perception of love is completely warped and limiting. I feel romantic love is limiting and selfish in many ways. To me, it feels like it's how I think about a person, or how they make me feel, and if they don't do these things, how could I love them in return? It's about the individual. For me, Universal love expands far beyond conditional love and lust. Universal love is more inclusive and unconditional. It's a beautiful place to aspire and create in one's life. It's something that I fall in and out of all the time.

Naturally, I'm sharing from my perspective, so don't believe a word I'm saying unless it feels true for you or you have done your own research. In general, I think society takes things at face value without digging a little deeper. I invite you to read on in the hope my experience in some way will inspire you to begin your inner exploration and continue to discover the beauty of your inner world -- your hero's journey back home from the head to the heart.

"I'm sorry, forgive me.
I love you, I am grateful."
~ Original Hawaiian Forgiveness Process

When I'm in my head, I feel I'm more open to fears of not being enough or being rejected, closed to new concepts and judgmental. The payoff is that I don't need to focus on what is alive and take ownership of it. Living in the heart, I feel I'm more grounded, accepting of others, open to new ideas. When I come from this heart space, even when I'm nervous or something doesn't feel right, I'm able to be honest with myself and express how I'm feeling from a place that is still. My mind is strong, especially if I've been triggered; my mind will butt in and play an open loop of what's wrong with a situation and it will play it repeatedly until it's resolved. I've found that Ho'oponopono, a powerful Hawaiian prayer of forgiveness, takes the pressure off the reactive mind. I often use it as a mantra allowing it to bring me back into my heart. With intense emotional triggers, if Ho'oponopono doesn't work, then I'll eat something. This generally keeps my mind quiet and brings contentment. Allowing time to pass is another tool that helps to remove or reduce emotional charges, so I that I can be more responsive than reactive.

As counter-intuitive as it may sound, unconditional universal love is what I'm most afraid of. I see that is true for most people. It's almost like my mind is scared of losing control and always wants to butt in and give its opinion. I'm not saying the mind is bad. It just gets in the way sometimes. This is one of the reasons I seek out heart-opening experiences; it also feels good. I find the more I do this, the easier it is to drop into my heart space and be the kind and loving person that I aspire to be.

I remember when Facebook first introduced the love heart emoji. When I 'love hearted' some posts of my male friends, there was this awkward feeling that I felt from some of them. There is a part of me that just wants to share the love with the whole world. I'm also aware that this makes many people feel uncomfortable. Naturally, it's becoming a more popular way of expressing your emotions and it's never been easier to test your boundaries of what you will accept emotionally. The beauty is you don't have to take what I'm sharing on face value. You can verify how loving you are at any given moment. You can be your own experiment; simply scroll down you're feed and see what it feels like to love heart a post. There is no right or wrong here; it's just a matter of testing your boundaries. I don't always feel like loving on a post. Sometimes it just feels safer to give the blue thumb. The point is, why not stretch yourself in a secure environment? You're looking for your setpoint -- the place that I emotionally return to and, wish to spend most of my time. Am I mostly loving, accepting and full of praise? Or am I grumpy, insecure, judgmental and critical most of the time? If it's the latter, then I know I'm in my head and that's the domain of irrational fears.

> **"Listen to the wind, it talks.**
> **Listen to the silence, it speaks.**
> **Listen to your heart, it knows."**
> ~ Native American Proverb

That's my cue to do a meditation, or some breath work; this changes my mental state and brings me into my heart. You can do this by earthing - standing on the grass with bare feet as you consciously connect with nature. Going for a walk in the woods or toiling in the garden are also great ways to ground yourself and connect with your highest potential. Anything that fills up your heart space and supports you in resetting your set point. The purpose is to expand your sense of self, your identity, the part of you that determines what is possible. What do you believe to be true that may not be true? It's useful to challenge your beliefs and trace them back to their origin. Many of our beliefs hold us back, giving us the illusion of safety. The pay off is we get to stay the same as crazy as that might sound.

"The fear of the unknown is genuine. I want my core beliefs and values to be a guiding light of infinite potential, allowing me to step into the unknown, embracing it whole heartily for this is the place of possibility."

Joseph Campbell, the famous American philosopher, professor of literature and the mentor to George Lucas, the creator of the classic Sci-Fi adventure series Star Wars, said, "The cave you fear to enter holds the treasure you seek." Dying to our old self so we can expand, increase, and access more of our hidden potential, enjoying new levels of inner freedom and expression. The ego death means to embark on what Joesph Campbell termed the 'Hero's Journey'-- embracing the unknown and saying goodbye to the stagnant predictability of everything familiar to us. This is how we are able to walk the path of fulfillment.

My heart loves adventure and trusting its wisdom has lead me to live a full life of travel, inner exploration and changing career paths in my mid-thirties.

"The soul loves expansion and growth; rarely will you find this by living the same life over and over again."

Sometimes life can be a real paradox, especially when the 'thing' you love to do is the very thing that you fear the most. I'm sure there is something, at least one thing in your life right now that you would love to do. Perhaps you have conveniently not gotten around to doing it, facing your fears around it or admitting that you've been avoiding doing it? May I ask what is stopping you? It can help if you imagine that your soul is trying to communicate to you through your intuition, that there is more to the life you're currently living. Could that be possible? I feel I'm mostly at a place now where the heart is a guiding light of wisdom, and all I need to do is listen and follow it to wherever I need to go.

> **"The mind doesn't know the way.**
> **The heart has been there,**
> **and the soul never left."**
> ~ Unknown

This wasn't always the case. I was afraid of my soul's calling: its stillness and power terrified me, not to mention the mind's desire to survive and thrive. Of course, I could distract myself on social media or through sports or some meaningless chores and pretend to have all the answers. I still do this, to be frank; it just feels like more of a choice that I'm consciously aware of. There is an acute sense of awareness that I'm off track. That wasn't always the case in the past. I wouldn't have the faintest idea that I was asleep to my potential and heart's desire. Eventually, when I had a little taste of my soul's presence, I'd get myself busy with 'important work' like earning a living and paying my bills or addressing any number of pains from my past. I use to think that if my past didn't happen to me, then I'd be ok. Now I feel that I have a deeper understanding of myself and I'll be ok because of what happened to me. I understand what I didn't want or what wasn't good for me before I became clear and gained clarity on what direction I wanted my life to take. It took many hard lessons and falls from grace, but as John Newton's song Amazing Grace goes, *I once was lost and now, I'm found, I once was blind, but now I see.* One of my favorite thought leaders, Dr. Wayne Dyer, used to say, "I'm better than I use to be." I can honestly say that I'm better than I used to be.

Let me rewind to a time when I was lost and felt unloved, so you have some context about my life. Firstly, I use to think that it was my parents that needed therapy, not me! If I just built this successful business and showed everyone how awesome and great I was, everything would be rosy. Through my traumas, my heart and soul awakened. Maybe that's not the case for everyone, but that's how this life played out for me. A series of isolated incidents created one big pain point from bullying, intimidation, physical abuse, verbal abuse, and sexual abuse all before I was ten. I remember one significant and very emotional event when I was seven years old sitting in front of the TV watching my favorite program, *Different Strokes*. I could easily lose myself in that show, and if I needed to go to the bathroom, I would hold off until an ad break and then high tail it to the toilet and whiz back before I would miss anything.

This particular Saturday afternoon, I was holding onto a number two, and as soon as the ads came on, off I went to take care of business. I made it back in time to watch the main character Arnold put his pet goldfish, Abraham, in the bathtub. I thought it was great until I heard my mother's boyfriend Phillip yelling out, "You filthy animal" as he came back into the lounge room!"

When I went to the bathroom earlier, a nugget of poo had fallen out onto the carpet in the hallway leading to the toilet and Phillip had trodden on it. He was furious. I was frozen like a rabbit caught in the headlights in the middle of the road, the ominous warning looming. Hearing the commotion, my mom came over from the kitchen on the other side of the lounge room to Phillip. Here I was sandwiched between the two, dumbfounded as what to do next. This was the first time that I had seen Phillip engulfed in anger, as he screamed his lungs dry through his long handlebar moustache. It also didn't help that he was six feet, eight inches tall and built like a brick shit house.

"Forgive those that didn't know how to love you. They were teaching you how to love yourself."
~Alex Ozil

My mom had an agitated looked on her face trying to work out what was going on. He quickly shouted, 'I've trodden on his shit on the way to the bathroom; what are we going to do about it?' To my dismay, my mom stammered, 'Rub his face in it like a dog so that he won't do it again.'

Before I could say a word, Phillip grabbed me by the ankle and pulled me swiftly along the carpet into the hallway. He then picked me up by the ankles and drove my head into the turd like a pole, again and again, dropping me to the floor. I was a bawling mess and was sent to my room where I cried uncontrollably for hours. Then my mom came into my room that I shared with my older brother. She had a stoic look on her face as she escorted me back to the bathroom and made me wash the shit out of my hair. I was still crying uncontrollably when I was sent back to my room. I felt this deep pain that shook me through to my core. Later, I came out for dinner and sat at the dining room table almost breathless from sobbing. I tried to eat in the uncomfortable silence of my family who all averted their eyes from me. That experience broke my heart. I was too young to realize the profound damage that had been done which caused me to form a wall around my heart. We believe the wall will protect us, heal us even, but it just makes it worse in my experience. The heart slowly dies of suffocation. I've spent most of my adult life dismantling that wall brick by brick so I can at least let the light in and heal the wound and make peace with it.

I don't know how you dealt with your childhood trauma, but I chose escapism. I did almost anything to escape reality. Daydreaming in class was a favorite. I used to love imagining I was somewhere else, instead of listening or learning about a subject that had no real bearing on my life. Being the class clown bought me a ticket out of reading or writing, and I enjoyed being a disturbing element. It wasn't until I lost my first business through drug addiction that I discovered there was an enormous amount of pain in my heart that I needed to deal with and resolve if I was ever going to succeed in getting my life back together. It's been an exciting ride learning how to trust my intuition, listen to my body and have enough trust within myself to follow my heart. I'm growing into the discovery that we are capable of so much more than we know.

"You always gain by giving love."
~ Reese Witherspoon

Now that I have gotten myself to a point where I no longer feel like a victim of my circumstances, that I'm in charge of my life and I can create my own destiny, being of service played a huge role in my life. It has helped my heart heal. Love, to me, is to be of service. I remember the first time I visited an orphanage, Hope Children's Home, in Dalung, Bali. Nestled in the back streets, it was a little hard to find, but I was greeted warmly by Wayan, the daughter of the founders. She had 30 odd children that were present who sang me a welcome song. It was an English Christian song of some sort. They were like a mini choir and I felt like their special guest.

During my visit, I met two university students from the U.K. They were doing a social science degree. The two young men had volunteered their time, helping around the home, spending time with the children. Although it was a mandatory requirement of their degree, they were mostly enjoying the experience. We ate a simple lunch of rice, vegetables, egg and tempe. After lunch, I helped the children do the dishes; they enjoyed my dancing, joking around and laughing. At one point, we all had a mini water fight which was great fun for all. I think the most important thing you can give anyone is your time, because that's all we have in life.

The experience with the children showed me that we are all emotionally equal -- we all have something valuable to share with the world if only we can transcend our hurt, fear, or pain long enough to focus on what's right in our lives. I feel we have a choice about what we focus on in any given moment; it's our consciousness that creates our reality. I was at the beach yesterday with my girlfriend, this is during the pandemic, while Bali is quite safe and chilled about it all there are still many places that are closed. We were sitting at a beach club on the east coast, having lunch after a long walk in the black volcanic sand. My girlfriend leans over and whispers that the man next to her smells, I looked over and I could see he had no shirt on and wore grubby shorts. He immediately senses that we are talking about him, causing him to tap his hand hard onto the table. I felt a bit awkward already because the beach club was only open to guests that were staying at the hotel. We kind of pretended we were staying there and walked straight into the restaurant like we owned the place.

My girlfriend continued to snuggle close to me while we looked at a group of boats out at sea. The man and his girlfriend spoke to each other in Indonesian, and it felt like they were talking about us. I look over and the guy is staring at me. I stare back, smile and say, 'Hi, how are you doing? Are you all alright?

He looks at my shorts like they're grubby and answers pointing at his girlfriend, 'She was just saying that I look like you, and you probably want to punch me like she wants to punch me.'

**"If we dive deep enough into ourselves,
we will find the one thread of universal
love that ties all beings together."**

~ Amma

We all laughed, agreeing that we do look alike. At
first, I thought he said I wanted to punch him. I think it
was a combination of his thick Italian accent, and me
already feeling a little uneasy. He said, 'I'm Italian
(making a repetitive gesture with his hand). I have my
unusual ways.' In a joking manner, I retorted with
'Yeah stop spreading corona.' We shared what felt
like an uncomfortable laugh and went back to
chatting with our respective partners.

I teased my girlfriend that I didn't feel comfortable
with sharing what she had mentioned about him and
his body odor, she responded with a bright blush
bringing a rose color to her cheeks and we laughed
together. When we got up to leave and paid the bill, I
said goodbye and wished them well, but there was
still a bit of tension in the air. I brushed it off with a
smile as they continued to stare unpleasantly. That
experience highlighted to me that what energy you
put out will be returned to you. Often you will receive
instant feedback that is a clear sign of your internal
state of being. Had we come from love, we would

have received love, but we came from judgment and that is what was returned straight back at us. If you would like more love in your life, be loving; if you want more respect, be respectful; it's a matter of being a reflection of what you want to be returned to you. My philosophy in a situation like this is to reflect on what went wrong and how I could approach things differently should I be faced with a similar situation in the future. No doubt if I saw him again, I would bring high vibes and build more of a connection with my Italian twin.

Seemingly bad things happen for no reason, without provocation or instigation; on the outside completely void of love. This is how I initially felt about my childhood trauma and significant events in my life that shook me to my core. It was done to me. Of course I'm the victim. I was innocent in all cases. How unfair? The victim outlook never brought me anything useful. Sure, there was sympathy, but where will that take you? I found the poor me hard-luck story breeds resentment, fear, shame, and a whole bunch of heavy emotions that can become negative imprints in your subconscious mind; it's like flypaper blocking your heart connection emotionally while reinforcing the wall. What served me well, was to recalibrate how I perceived my trauma so that I didn't just to see the negative experiences, but also the positive learnings that came from those events. Did it make you mentally stronger? Build resilience? I had to work with a professional to find my positive traits that came out of that incident with my mother's then-boyfriend, recalibrating the event. That victimhood mindset had a hold on me hard, but once I could see from both vantage points, I was able to change the way I viewed the experience. I felt free. A tear of gratitude rolled down my cheek as my heart filled with love for my mom or momzie as I like to call her. As strange as it may sound, I wouldn't change that experience for anything in the world. It taught me resilience, determination, forgiveness, and how to be heart-centered and tenacious in the pursuit of my dreams.

> **"Seek opportunities to put more love
> into the world."**
> ~ Marianne Williamson

I don't think you ever really heal your wounds. I've accepted them and I allow myself to be humble enough to be compassionate for the challenges that other people might be going through. One thing I don't do is let the story control me as much as it used to. I look for heart-opening experiences, like volunteering my time at Hope Children's Home. The day after my first visit was such a heart-expanding moment. Spending time with the children playing games after we did the dishes, impacted me deeply. I played soccer with the boys and they taught me how to count in Indonesian. There was one little child in particular who was so sad; she must have only been three or four years old. This little girl was sitting on the concrete floor by herself while the other children were playing hopscotch, and hand slapping games as they sang songs and ran around the place joyfully. I said hello to her, no response, so I picked her up and placed her on my shoulders with a leg on either side of my head. I began to dance to the song a group of girls had started to sing. Soon enough, other children joined in, laughing and just being silly. I had the little girl by her hands and I was moving them up and down. After a few minutes, I placed her back on the ground and she gave me a little shy smile.

The next day I felt a heaviness in my heart. The afternoon at the children's home had brought up a lot of stuff around my abandonment issues as a child. I gave myself the gift of being with my sadness that was welling up deep within. I even cried a few tears releasing the pain I had stored within my heart from many years ago. I silently thanked the children in my mind's eye for allowing me to be there for them. Over the years, I visited the Hope Children's Home on several occasions, even taking my then-girlfriend and a friend who had ridden her scooter into a tree only a couple of weeks earlier, causing serious damage to her leg. After spending two weeks in the hospital, visiting the children's home was her first trip out of the hospital. Later, she told me that it was one of the best experiences she'd ever had in her life. It touched her so profoundly, helping her to forget about her situation at the time.

Resetting my set point became more manageable once I flushed out the accumulation of unconscious fears that I was hanging onto. I do this regularly. The result is that I'm more centered in heart-based intelligence. That doesn't mean I don't have challenges, although now I feel like I'm able to respond with more compassion and understanding. I believe that our level of empathy increases and the bounce of the ball goes our way more often than not. This, to me, is universal love -- it's not just for the select few; it's omnipresent, available anywhere and anytime you are open to connecting with it.

You always have a choice, you can come from fear, or you can choose love; the choice is yours.

"A miracle is a shift
in perception from
fear to love."

~ Marianne Williamson

CHAPTER FOUR

❖

You Carry So Much Love In Your Heart; Give Some To Yourself

By Beth Ranchez

"Love yourself enough to set boundaries. Your time and energy are precious. You get to choose how you use it. You teach people how to treat you by deciding what you will and won't accept."
~ Anne Taylor

…and this is precisely what I did after my major accident late last year - on December 7th, 2019. A near-death experience that changed my life forever!

I have always been very disciplined when it comes to self-care. My upbringing and the values shared by my parents taught me the importance of balance and looking after my own needs without being selfish. You cannot give from an empty well, and for me, prioritizing a healthy mind and body are daily practices, just like my faith.

I am grateful for all the experiences in my life, the good and the bad. They made me the person I am today: resilient, strong, and keeping a solid belief in the goodness of people. I always have hope and am gifted with the ability to still see light at the end of the tunnel, and I never lose sight of the bigger picture.

My Life, Habits & Gratitude

As the eldest of five, and brought up on our farm, love was not just a word but a daily experience; it was an exercise of activities practiced by my parents, who without any doubt, showed and instilled in us gratitude and unconditional love. They demonstrated love for each other, love for the land, and appreciation and love for God's blessings. My dad especially made us aware of the abundance provided by nature. My mom showed us how to care for our bodies, the importance of nurturing ourselves and others, and about eating healthy food produced by the gifts of our land. Still, if I close my eyes, I can see and even smell the beautiful fresh multi-colored fruits from the many trees surrounding our home.

Healthy habits were a natural way of living at our home. My mom always made us eat a nutritious breakfast before we left the house. And exercise was also part of our daily routine. We did not need an app to get up and do our regular exercises; we just knew that, after getting out of bed, the best way to start our day was by stretching our bodies and stilling our minds, like meditation. We were taught to listen to our bodies, to experience the moment, not to rush but to enjoy and live every second of our lives to the fullest.

I still start my days with this simple routine. I fully believe that not having a set daily routine and just winging your day creates stress and anxiety. Like my mom, I always carefully design a method that works best for me, one which helps me to be productive, in control, and to be the best person I can be. I have learned that designing and adhering to a personal daily routine is the path to freedom, productivity, happiness, and fulfilling my true potential.

Part of my daily routine is also journaling appreciation, acknowledgment, and understanding of how I became the person I am today, and I often recall the time when I was a young girl living at home. These memories always fill me with love and excitement. I am so incredibly blessed. Farm life, the wisdom shared by my parents and grandparents, and the simplicity of that early stage of my life remind me of what happiness is all about. Especially during challenging times in my life, this practice gives me strength and has been proven to be a recipe for happiness. A few years ago, as part of my journey to self-love, I started my own gratitude practice. It has had more of a positive impact on my life than any other decision I've ever made.

Prior to adopting gratitude, I was going through a difficult time in my life. I had some challenging relationships, family members battling with disease, and I wasn't taking very good care of myself. I was caught in the familiar trap of eating badly, not exercising much, and working too hard, and I often felt tired and overwhelmed.

Knowing that I needed to make some changes in my life but not really sure where to start, I noticed that I was seeing the word gratitude everywhere I went. Seeing this word so often grabbed my attention and I was intrigued. Despite my scepticism that something as simple as expressing appreciation could make a difference to my state of mind, I was curious enough to give it a try. Over time I was humbled and amazed by the impact that focusing on gratitude began to have on my life. Day by day, I felt calmer and more at peace. Since I started this journey of gratitude, the benefits continue to grow and flourish, making it a very important part of my daily routine.

> **"Six best doctors in the world:**
> **Sunlight**
> **Rest**
> **Exercise**
> **Diet**
> **Gratitude**
> **Friends**
> **Maintain them in all stages in life and enjoy a healthy life."**
> - Steve Jobs

My Purpose: A Life of Constant Learning

Now, please allow me to indulge and tell you my story, my blessings, and my challenges; this is the story I would one day like for my grandchildren to tell their grandchildren—my history and my legacy.

My siblings and I went to a public school. We walked there, a daily three-kilometer exercise that set us up for a day dedicated to learning. Knowledge has always been a highway to success and happiness in my life.

Determined to always better myself and focus on learning, I graduated as class valedictorian and topped the National College Entrance Examination; hence, I was automatically admitted to the university with a full scholarship. This was a great achievement, as attending college in my country is very expensive, and this eased the financial burden on my parents.

After I finished my Bachelor of Arts in Economics, I started to experiment with the art of soif de vivre, enjoying the finer things in life. I enjoyed spending time with my friends and going to parties. I also loved my own company, reading, designing clothes, birdwatching, and, most of all, I started to develop an appreciation for music.

A few weeks after my graduation, I was offered my first job as a researcher for a small company. This involved traveling and meeting different types of people. It opened up new experiences, new opportunities, and required me to step out of my comfort zone. I loved every minute of it. I especially loved the travel and the exposure to new and exciting environments; it almost didn't feel like a job. I had so much fun and learned a lot about life and living it to the fullest.

The job gave me new connections that led me to my next career move. I was offered a new role for an engineering executive account company as a marketing executive. I, again, thoroughly enjoyed the travel to exciting places and meeting a variety of interesting people, such as company directors, safety and HR managers, and accountants. All of these people showed me their perspectives of work and life. I absorbed their knowledge and experiences like a sponge and strengthened my understanding of my own purpose.

I constantly felt a desperate need to move on. I wanted more and more, and after nearly two years of working in marketing, I joined the Armed Forces of the Philippines as a researcher. This move eventually let me immigrate to Australia. I had to spread my wings and be courageous. I needed to take a chance; there was just no stopping me.

Like it was yesterday, I recall landing at the Tullamarine Airport in Melbourne on a sunny spring morning in October 1986. I had a few hours before boarding my flight to Sydney, a place I would call home for many years, although at that time everything felt alien. However, I knew with every bone in my body that this was the start of a new journey that would bring me closer to my purpose and closer to my destiny.

When I finally arrived in Sydney, I was convinced all my prayers were heard. Sydney was a beautiful dream come true, and I had to pinch myself to believe I actually could call this amazing place my home. The Harbour Bridge, Opera House, and the Sydney Tower, places that I had only seen on postcards, were right there in my new city and I knew that I was destined to be here.

Determined not to get distracted, I put on my smile and walking shoes and set out to make friends and find a job! Fifteen days after I arrived in Sydney, I landed a job working for a timeshare company with an amazing Canadian couple. I quickly adapted to the Australian way of living. I was 100% dedicated to my work and to learning every day from these amazing people, who helped me to truly settle in this big country, Down Under.

My job gave me opportunities and exposure to develop and improve myself. During my career, I have been blessed to work with some thought-provoking organizations, which resulted in us moving to Perth, my home for the last 25 years. Arriving in the most isolated city in the world actually made me feel connected and at home; it felt like I truly belonged to Western Australia. I continued working in the finance industry and I loved my work.

My first boss in Perth was a true inspiration, and he became my mentor and encouraged me to start studying again. With his support and encouragement, I became a qualified financial planner, and this led me to my next career move. I joined one of the biggest banks in Australia (ANZ) in the Retail Financial Planning Department.

Looking back at this crazy time, I combined a full-time job with full-time study, while also being a full-time mom, but I loved every minute of it. I was on fire and felt that nothing could stop me. Life was perfect.

My career at the bank evolved and after nine months of working with two amazing senior financial planners, I moved into the private banking world. I loved the exposure, although I also became acutely aware of the job challenges and demands. And the hours were long. It all resulted in a neglect of my health and well-being. I started to lose weight and felt depressed.

As mentioned earlier in my story, I am blessed with hope and faith. I believe that the universe knew I was struggling and therefore intervened.

A new opportunity was presented to me when I received a very unexpected call from one of the other major banks, Commonwealth Bank of Australia (CBA), offering me a similar position but in a different environment. It was simply an offer I could not refuse, and this opportunity turned out to be an absolute gift from the heavens.

I am proud to say that I worked for CBA for more than eleven years and left the company in March 2018 with mixed emotions; but like everything in life, good things come to an end, and when one door closes, another one opens.

Since my retirement from the big banks, I allowed myself to be of service to others. I felt it was my time to give back to society. I dedicated my time to working as a volunteer, to coaching and helping less fortunate people. I'm blessed with so many gifts, and I felt like it was the right time to invest in others, to coach them to happiness and fulfillment and to make them believe in themselves as my parents had taught me to always believe in God and myself.

I also regained a renewed passion for my birth country, the Philippines. I recently took my daughter there; this beautiful country is part of her roots, and I felt blessed and proud to introduce her to her heritage.

I had not been back home since my dad passed away in 2014, so you can understand my excitement traveling with my daughter and taking her on this historic journey. And I could hardly wait to re-introduce my beautiful daughter to my mom and childhood friends. My daughter was glowing all the time. Getting to know her family more intimately was like filling in the missing puzzle pieces in her life. I was so honored to see how she devoured the stories, the atmosphere, and the history, knowing that all of this was part of her life, too. I was humbled to see her interest in getting to know me better by understanding my past.

The most significant gift during our time in the Philippines was flying into Isabela Province with my daughter. This is where I was born and raised; this is the place that oozes with beautiful memories, the place that truly created me.

As you can imagine, the meeting between my daughter, Ashleigh, and my mom was very emotional for all of us.

Reuniting with My Mom – Returning to Love and Embracing Wisdom

My beautiful, amazing and wise mom taught my daughter, like she taught me before, the lessons that are important in life. She told me that we all have unique gifts and talents and that we should embrace everything unique about ourselves. She said to my daughter:

"As you grow up, you will come to know these talents and you will develop passions and understand the purpose of your life, and goals that you want to accomplish. If you want to be a painter, then paint. If you're going to be a teacher, then teach. If you're going to be an entrepreneur, then do that. Decide what is important to you and do it."

However, Whatever You Do – Throw Your Heart into It

"Whatever you decide to do, you must put your whole self into it. Don't hold back on love, relationships, work, and involvement in your community or avocations. Give it your all. Take the brakes off and embrace your life and all that you do. You will find that it makes life so much more fun, and you will get so much more out of it."

No Matter What Happens to You
– Take Responsibility for It

"Even if it wasn't your fault—especially if it wasn't your fault—take responsibility for fixing it. Life has a way of bringing all of us a great deal of happiness, but it also has a way of hurting us.

"No matter what has happened, it is up to you to resolve it. It is up to you to envision what should occur next and to put a plan in place to make it happen.

"If you take responsibility and control, you will imagine new possibilities and design something that you do want for yourself. You will take yourself out of the past and move yourself to a better place. This will make a profound difference in your life. You will be happier with your opportunities, your support systems, and your environment."

Be a Lifelong Learner

"Always be open to learning new things. Be curious about the people, the experiences, the events and discoveries taking place in the present as well as those things that we can learn from in the past. Decide to continually understand the world around you and expand your thinking and ways of doing things.

"Take classes, attend lectures, read books (just like your mom always did) and hang out with others who are interested in what you are. Be engaged. You will find that your life is more interesting, you will have greater opportunities, and *you will never be bored."*

There Are Beautiful People Everywhere

"I have never moved to different places, like your mom, but from her travels, I have learned that there are amazing people everywhere. There is always a sense of sadness when you leave the familiar and replace it with the unfamiliar. It is hard saying goodbye to friends, acquaintances, and support systems. It is challenging to start fresh and to meet new people. But learn from your mother; be inspired by her drive and spirit, and discover people who will inspire you and with whom you will develop a close friendship. You will find people who you will love and who will love you. There are beautiful people, no matter where you go. And when you develop a friendship with them, it will feel like you have always known them.

"There will be some people who will take some time to get to know and others that you will be good friends with right from the start.

"Always be open to what can happen and you will find them."

Expect the Best

"Say yes to life and be open to new experiences. You may not always get what you want, but you will generally get what you expect."

Laugh Often

"Have a great sense of humor. Laughing has a healing effect on you, both mentally and physically. We create so many of our problems by taking it all too seriously. Move through this life lightly and take care of yourself; create the experience that you treasure. And laugh."

Don't Forget Your Connection to All of Nature

"There is a force, an energy that we share, and it is the power that connects us all. It is the Source that we all came from and it is the energy that we will all return to when we die. Don't ever forget that you are part of something spiritual and eternal."

Make the World a Better Place

"There is so much prejudice, criticism, and judgment in this world. Never do anything to add to this negativity. Use your natural gifts and talents to make the world a better place.

"It is a beautiful life—live it!"

My daughter will recall this conversation and the imparted wisdom from my mom for many years to come, and it has made us both into better people, always striving to excel, always wanting to be more, to make things better for ourselves and others.

The Journey of Returning to Love in My Life

Ashleigh will never forget this special time with her grandma, and I hope and pray that one day she will pass this wisdom of pure love on to her children and her children's children like I and my family have done before her.

During the trip home, I made myself a promise, a promise never to lose sight of the bigger picture—to dedicate my life to love and always, with God's help, be of service. This is my reason for being, and following in the footsteps of my parents, this is what gives me the greatest joy and fulfillment. Sometimes through events and challenges in our lives, we go off track. We get distracted and challenged, and we forget who we indeed are; we forget our values, our purpose, and what we were meant to do in this world. Like my mom said, you need to live with your heart open, not closed!

Taking the first step back on my track, I accepted an invitation to deliver an inspirational speech for the Year 6 graduation ceremony at my alma mater for the class of 2018-2019. It was such an honor to be in front of these amazing students, who were taking the first steps entering into another stage of life: *the real world.* I took pride in reminding these eager minds that we often forget, or take for granted, the most obvious things around us. Going to high school is about learning how to think, exercising some degree of control over your thoughts so that you can choose what to pay attention to in your reality. Our thoughts affect our realities, and the ability to decide how you construct meaning from experience will determine the lenses from which you see the world and how you react in return. Knowledge is power, and combined with working hard and being kind, you will see that amazing things will happen.

At that moment, it was my turn to give back and inspire the younger generations for a better future.

Love - Reconnected

"Love is what we are born with innately. Fear is what we learn. The spiritual journey is the unlearning of fear and prejudices and the acceptance of love back in our hearts. Love is the essential reality and our purpose on earth. To be consciously aware of it, to experience love in ourselves and others, is the meaning of life. Meaning does not lie in things. Meaning lies in us."
~ Marianne Williamson

The trip to the Philippines was like a spiritual retreat, reconnecting me with my heritage, with love, with my values, and reconnecting me with my purpose.

Determined to continue this path, I accepted a VIP invitation from Jefferson Santos, author, speaker and trainer, to join him and his team in Kuala Lumpur, Malaysia, for a three-day Leadership Boot Camp. It was an experience I will never forget. The timing was perfect and I enjoyed this camp, receiving the right tools together with the mindset to transform and create my ideal life again. I had let life happen to me, and my mom's wisdom made me realize the need to connect back with love and to integrate this in my daily life so that I could continue to embark on my spiritual path and receive the guidance to take my life to the next level. I realized, as I mentioned in my graduation speech, that I could create everything from within, and I needed to connect again with my inner self. I needed to reinvest in my relationship with life by increasingly engaging from a love imperative.

"Cultivating loving kindness for ourselves is the foundation of real love for our friends and family, for new people we encounter in our daily lives, for all beings and for life itself."
~ Sharon Salzberg

Homecoming

I also realized that my *retirement* was temporary and just a stepping stone to the next phase in my life. I was excited to explore what is next without being in a rush. I enjoyed playing around in my head with different options and opportunities, and when I received a call to attend an interview for a position with a small finance company, I accepted it and met with the company director and the senior financial planner. Shortly afterward, I joined this organization and enjoyed being back in the workforce again. However, within weeks I was back to my old self, still working late, skipping lunch, compromising some of my values, and feeling depressed. I did not get enough sleep; I felt pressured all the time and then **it** happened.

It was on a Friday. I went to work early, had no time for lunch, and stayed until late to finish my work before heading home for the weekend. I received a call from two friends who asked if I wanted to join them for a drink. I decided I needed a lift, and spending time with the girls would just put me in the right mindset to start the weekend. I joined them, and I was right: I felt better again.

We laughed, talked, and listened to a live band playing fantastic music. After a while, I told my friends I wanted to go home. I was tired from the week of working hard and was looking forward to going to bed and getting some rest. I picked up my car from my friend's place and drove home. It was almost midnight. The freeway was not busy around that time, and it was an easy drive home. I put on my music and my cruise control so that I would not accidentally speed, and I was on my way. This was my last recollection, as suddenly I heard these loud noises and could feel my car spinning and hitting something. Then everything went blank.

When I opened my eyes, I did not know where I was. All I could see was this huge airbag in my face. And I realized what had happened. I had fallen asleep while driving my car. My first reaction was to check to see if I was injured. I checked my arms and my legs, and thankfully I could still feel them and move them. I tried to open my door, but it was stuck and I could not get out. Then I realized that I had to get out, because my car could explode with me in it. I can safely say that I have never felt so vulnerable and so scared in my entire life.

I am not sure where my strength came from, but I finally managed to get out of the car. I was in shock and devastated. I just stood for a few seconds and then took a photo of my wrecked car for the insurance claim. Then a car stopped and a kind man asked me if I was okay. I was in a daze, and this Good Samaritan called the police and the ambulance and stayed with me until they arrived. The ambulance was there in no time, and these amazingly brave and kind people looked after me. The police and a tow truck were at the scene soon afterward and looked after my car.

That night I had two guardian angels looking after me. The swift response from the Samaritan most likely saved my life and my angel in heaven decided that it was not yet my time.

This, however, clearly was a wake-up call. I was lucky that I escaped with just a few bruises and a sore arm. However, the emotional pain after five months is still there. I did go back to work after five days of sick leave. The company I worked for showed no compassion, on the contrary actually; they instructed me not to take too much time off as they could not afford to have me away from the office.

In some ways, this was a blessing. I had to learn the lessons from this event, this wake-up call. It was so easy for me to fall back into life, and not align with my values. I believe that it was the universe that sent me a significant message. Initially, there were the small messages I had ignored, like feeling tired all the time and being unwell and depressed. And, as I continued to ignore these signs, I believe the universe had to shake me into action, literally and figuratively.

That day, I handed in my notice of resignation. I realized this was not my destiny and I had to go back to a more balanced and healthy life.

Today, I practice yoga again at least three times a week. I do Pilates, body balance, eating healthy meals, and going for long walks with my friends. I spend special times with my family and enjoy my two little dogs, the simple things in life, and the essential things in life!

The car accident has changed my perspective. I forgot about the important things, such as time with my loved ones, time for me, time to reflect, time to share with people who have less, and time to give back to our community. I forgot the lessons my mom so beautifully taught me and had only recently shared with my daughter.

Now my life is simple, and although the accident was devastating, I am grateful, as it made me wake up. It made me remember to smell the roses again, to appreciate the gifts of life, and to appreciate my family and my friends. You only live once, and life is tragically short. The older I get, the more I realize that happiness takes work. People who smile in public have been through every bit as much as people who cry, frown, and scream. They just have the courage and strength to smile through it anyway.

I have decided to follow a new set of rules for myself. Going forward, these are my guidelines.

- **Only do what's important.** It doesn't matter what it is; I will do what makes me happy. Everything else will fall into place.

- **Take risks, a lot of them** – so I will never have regrets.

- **Live in the present.** My past is important to learn from, but my future is vital; I will work towards the best outcome for everyone. At the end of the day, though, the only thing that exists outside of my head is the present. So, I will think about my past and future, but only dwell on the present.

- **Ignore the haters.** There will always be someone around to point out the many ways I will fail. I know that every winner loses, but not every loser wins. Successful people don't start successfully. What makes them successful is that they keep pushing through failure.

- **Don't compromise my values.** If something doesn't feel right, I don't do it. I will not compromise on my internal code of ethics. I will trust my instincts. I will do whatever I want, so long as I can look at myself in the mirror.

- **Do charitable acts for others.** It is so easy to make a difference, even if I do one small act of kindness per day.

- **Keep an open mind.** Just because I think I am right about something doesn't mean there aren't other ways to look at it. I will listen to ideas I don't agree with or understand; this keeps my brain active and healthy.

- **Speak through my actions.** Live healthy by being active, eating well, and walking my talk all the time.

- **Love, love, love, love - Tell people I love them, every day** — my family, strangers, friends, and myself. I am just going for it. I have nothing to lose!!

"Cherish every moment and every person in your life, because you never know when it will be the last time you see someone."

~ Unknown

"Get out of your head and
get into your heart.
Think less and feel more."

~ Osho

CHAPTER FIVE

❖

My Journey to Self-Love Mastery

By Debi Beebe

I t was fifteen years ago when I found myself in the middle of a complete meltdown; a total breakdown. I was having the ugliest cry in the middle of the hallway with my family staring at me as if I had lost my mind.

No one came near me. I was showing up in the rawest form of hurt. At that moment, I was not the perfect person, the composed level-headed person, the approachable person I was brought up to be — not even a little bit. So, they didn't approach me. I cried overwhelming, intense and very present pain. I had a realization that these emotions connected back to being abandoned as a child.

"Knock, knock"
"Who's there?"
"Your abandonment issues."

I was feeling more unloved than I'd ever felt in my life. Again, "Knock, knock."

Begrudgingly, I answered, "Who's there?"

"No one who wants to love, assure, hug, or help you. Remember? You don't deserve any of that."

What?! Are you freakin' kidding me? How did I never understand this before now?! I had never given a name to what happened, and up until this point, I had never even thought about it.

"Look at you, standing there being a mess. They have no idea how to help you. Heck, I'll prove to them that I'm deserving of their time and love," I thought.

It was late, they were going to bed, and I was alone.

There was a swirly kind of quietness that seared through my soul. I questioned myself in deep, dark stillness. Why did I deserve love?

When I was four years old, I saw my biological dad for the last time. My parents were getting divorced and they thought it would be best if he stayed away. A couple of years later, my mom remarried a man who adopted me, only to leave me (us) when I was 14.

On top of that I never saw or had a relationship with my real father; he died when I was only 22 years old.

At the time of his death, his parents and two sisters were still living. I had no contact with them until I decided to look for the people who never looked for me.

When I was a teenager, I tried looking for my dad. I thought that every man that looked nice or looked like me, could it be him? I would search their faces -- faces of strangers, thinking to myself, "Wow what if that was my Dad?"

I would celebrate Father's Day with silent sadness again thinking or even talking to myself, "Hey Happy Father's Day! Even if I don't have one...."

But it was okay, I was tough, strong and didn't need anyone. I had my Mom, my maternal grandparents and that was enough. Until it wasn't.

I married my high school sweetheart right out of high school and became a mom at age 18. We had our second child when I was 22. My husband had always promised me we would find my dad, but my dad passed away five months after the birth of my second child.

Over the years, I often continued to pay tribute to Father's Day. I would think of my dad and hoped that he was enjoying Heaven. Usually, I always tried not to think about never really having a dad.

After our kids had grown and moved out, my husband thought it would be a good idea to look for anyone in my dad's family. I sent out postcards to any address that I could find. I thought the postcards were a good idea in case a nosey neighbor got the mail and might know something about my father and give me a call. I received no responses. Somehow, we found a phone number of somebody in another state that was a relative that knew my paternal grandmother. With my hopes running high, I made the call and she let me know that my grandmother had passed away the year before. I felt a great sadness in my heart that I had started my search a little too late. The woman told me that one of my dad's sisters was still living, and gave me her number. As I dialed my Aunt's phone number, I had a sinking feeling in my gut. I was afraid of rejection and more abandonment. Would I be accepted? Why didn't they look for me?

She answered the phone to my surprise and we made arrangements to meet the next day. She lived in a ranch like neighborhood in San Diego two hours from me.

It was crazy. It was weird, but nice. There was love. And there was me. We spent the day together and I learned that I had lots and lots of cousins and there was going to be a family reunion the following weekend. Of course we would attend, no matter how uncomfortable I was feeling.

Here I am an adult, with my own adult children and a granddaughter. My Aunt and all the cousins had so many stories and memories of my dad and how fun he was. It was so wonderful to meet people that I was related to. We had many resemblances. They were nice, kind, loving and welcoming.

They told me about all the fun times they had with my dad, which hurt so much, because I didn't have any of that. Their stories of the good times, always ended with, "You're just like your dad - - funny, smart, charming, and the life of the party. He loved you so much."

That night (15 years ago) back at my daughter's house, in the middle of the hallway, I turned to look through the bedroom door at my beautiful grand-baby. As she lay there sleeping, my heart filled with great sadness, "How could anybody leave a beautiful innocent child?" If my Dad loved me so much, how could he leave me? I was a beautiful innocent child.

"If he loved me so much," I screamed, "how could he leave his beautiful baby?!"

At this moment, I felt emotionally out of control. I was deeply hurt and I felt unlovable, my tears flowed nonstop, I was exhausted and out of breath as I stood there just wanting someone to hug me. My family didn't approach me. I was abandoned emotionally and physically — again.

When reading my story, please know that my account has nothing to do with blaming someone else. I love my family dearly and they love me. No-one was prepared for the night that I had my realization. There were no tools at that point for any of us. No one ever knew anything was wrong. How could they have known? I needed to be perfect and in control. This story is a personal discovery of how I got to where I am today. This is my perspective, and everyone involved has their own viewpoint. In anyone's life, at any time, in any given situation, someone can try to do their absolute loving best, but that can turn into the total opposite experience for the person on the receiving end.

As I write this story, I wish you could feel the pain and the a-ha moments I had.

Throughout my whole life, I thought that if I didn't know about the bad times, or think about them, that was indeed the way to be healed. I thought that if I just smiled, laughed, loved, thought positive things, and said appreciative words, then I would be loved. Then, and only then, I would be hugged. Anything less than a perfect version of myself meant I didn't deserve anything at all.

I had built the biggest wall of coping mechanisms, so much so, that I never even thought of being unloved or abandoned. How could I? That would hurt too much. Instead, I practiced every day to be perfect; wearing makeup, smiling, saying the right things, and never letting anyone know how much it hurt that I was left behind.

I had no idea that deserving was a part of self-love. Every one of us deserves love. We are all worthy of that. I am enough. You are enough.

When I sat down to write this chapter, I really thought it would be easy to explain how to love oneself. As it turned out, it was much harder than I had imagined. When I thought about the question: "What is self-love?" that moment of truth was staring right back at me. The word I loathe, "vulnerability" was front and center. Am I worthy? Better yet, why do I deserve to write about self-love?

My mind quickly began to become overloaded with thoughts that there is just too much going on in my life. I am not enough. I have a business to run and people to help. I am not enough. My health seems to be a battlefield and I have no energy. I am not enough. I am disgusted with my body and I am fighting sadness and regret. I am not enough.

There are so many layers in my journey to self -love. As you read through, know that you deserve to find your own layers. Maybe you have fewer layers, maybe more? Perhaps you are just here to read something that could help someone else? Chances are, you are here reading this for yourself, just as much as I am here writing for myself. Originally, I had left out the word "deserve" in this chapter, probably because the recovering perfectionist in me still has some work to do. Work, indeed. Deserve means "to be worthy," and worthy means to have worth or value.

Time To Leave The Party

I am fun and I love people. Just watch. Watch me smile and laugh, be interesting, listen hard, lean in, be charming and wag my tail. Seriously, I am like a runt trying to nurse on its mama. That was me: "Like me. Love me. I am nice. I will be your best friend. Just accept me. Love me."

Oh, believe me, I have friends and people who like and love me. However, do you ever find yourself at work, social events, parties or even at your own family get-togethers and feel like you are not enough and nothing you say or do gets you any of the attention or love you are seeking? Inside you are begging, "See me. Love me. Understand me, please. I am lonely. Why aren't I enough?"

Time to leave the party. What does that even mean?

Time to leave the party for me was all about perfectionism, people-pleasing, and being who they expected me to be. I just could not deliver. So, of course, I would stay at the party until the very end, trying my hardest to be liked and accepted instead of just showing up and being me. There was clearly no self-love there. I wasn't showing up for me. I was showing up for others, and the more I stayed in that position, the more miserable I became. It was exhausting. I would walk away feeling gross. This was not who I wanted to show up as. This was my coping mechanism. I learned to be perfect and people pleasing, and I wasn't allowed to show up any differently.

What did I want? I wanted to feel close, connected, understood, supported, justified, important, worthy, and that I mattered to them. First, I had to matter to me. I had to leave the party.

Self-Love Mastery

I've waited for you to show up, to be here now, to love me and see.

Feel the sun and stroke my face, hear my heart and feel the pace.

The earth moves in the patterns as it must; see me now and feel the lust, the play, the search.

Just for me, I've waited for you to show up. To be here now, to dance, sing and write. To be still to watch the clouds and hear my heart pound.

I've waited for you to show up to be here and see-
I want to love you,
I mean,
me.
- Debi Beebe

Self-love requires mastery — knowing and being comfortable with what you want for you. A mastery of anything takes time. It is a journey, always a work in progress to learn, teach, and use the tools. When we stop people-pleasing, others might try to shame us simply because they think our life should look a certain way. This is where the mastery comes in. Self-love can look very different from person to person. We are all different, and we all have our own challenges.

Maybe you have felt like me and thought, "Self-love? Are you going to tell me to light a candle, meditate, and take a bubble bath?" My answer would be, No, but if that works for you, then, sure. But it will take more than a bubble bath."

On my path to self-love, there is a haunting thought that echoes and reminds me that "self-love exposes how you show up and love others."

Can I get an "Ouch!" and an "Amen!"? Think about it, you can only extend the amount of what you believe about yourself to others; we are affected by not doing the work -- the work of understanding ourselves and what drives us. For me I learned early on that I must show up in perfection and do everything with perfection otherwise I will not be loved. I knew that I had to keep complete control in as many areas of my life as possible. So maybe the question is not a question at all? Perhaps it is just understanding what self-love is not.

Here are some ideas of **what self-love isn't:**

Self-love is not settling for less than you deserve.

Self-love is not hurting yourself.

Self-love is not allowing others to mistreat you, no matter the time invested in the relationship.

Self-love is not polluting oneself with drugs and alcohol.

Self-love is not giving away your own beautiful power.

Toxicity is not self-love. Toxins come in all forms — from the environment and people you surround yourself with, to the very foods you eat — the ones that make you feel better in the moment and cover up the hurt.

Self-loathing is not self-love. You are beautifully and wonderfully made. In fact, self-loathing on some level is a question of, "Why are you punishing yourself?"

Keeping negative people around is not self-love. The relationships you keep for convenience end up harming you more than you could ever help them in return. Respect yourself enough to walk away if it does not feel good or right for you.

Learn to release everybody's expectations or judgments. Do not follow just because someone says so. How else will you find your own true self — your very own self-love?

Have you ever had to fight for something you wanted? Sometimes learning to love yourself takes some fighting for. Loving others isn't always easy. People have different mindsets, perspectives, goals, dreams, and plans, yet you still fight to keep the love alive. So why would fighting to keeping the love alive for yourself be any different?

We could end right there, right? Well, again, I am going to say "No." To truly learn anything worth learning, you must take a long look at it. Especially love. Self-love.

Part of my self-love journey was learning to be vulnerable. Learning to trust others. Learning that I am not in control of others. In fact, my need for controlling people or relationships is very much a part of what my own learned behavior, which goes hand in hand with my dad walking away. I built the need to control any situation so I would not be blindsided if someone left. Learning and embracing the stories, the lives, the lessons of the people who have formed and been a part of my life, actually made me learn to love myself, even when there was seemingly no one around to love me. I had to learn to embrace the child inside and her perspective of being abandoned and hurt.

To find self-love, I really had to understand this.

One of the ways I soothe myself and give way to letting go of the control I never really had, is looking from a different perspective. Choosing a story that serves me. When I am feeling uptight or feeling unloved by others, I tell myself this: "There is always a bigger picture."
Let me give you an example:
A couple of words that are similar to abandonment are Surrender and Rejection.

I get to choose the word that feels loving to me. And I feel that is okay. We can make up any story, why not for the better? I get to choose. I wasn't there. Surrender. Did my dad surrender his parental rights so that I might have a better life? Or Rejection. Did my dad walk away because I was an inconvenience? I get to choose the story. There is no way to know the truth. All things are truth. And maybe, just maybe him walking away was true Love.

Ultimate sacrifice and this love sacrifice was what led me to become the person I am today. I am strong. I am wise. I love people. I am fun. And I never want to leave anyone behind. I want everyone I come in contact with, to know that they matter and are worth everything -- they are loved.

Perfectionism showed up along the way with her friends: Control, Unworthy and Not Enough. I greeted them and I let them in. I learned from them. I sent them on their way and every once in a while, they come back and visit. We have coffee, we reminisce and they move on. They'll be back, but it is okay; they remind me that I am okay and I love me.

And my Aunt? She is a solid in my life. She is family and we spend as much time together as we can.

You will have your own beautiful story. You deserve it.

We all have stories. It is what connects us. Have you ever thought about yours? Have you ever started a journal? If you were to write about yourself, what you desire, your thoughts or even what you want to change, here is my suggestion. Gather your thoughts. Write your heart out all over a page about self-love. Share what that looks like for you. Then, you will start to understand more about yourself and what feels right for you. Be specific and very clear on what will not serve you in your self-love journey. Choose the words that feel loving to you and for you. Change your perspective. Remember you get to choose.

This has now become a journey for me in which I understand more as I learn and teach myself.

Self-love is having a regard for one's well-being and happiness. It means taking care of your own needs and not sacrificing your well-being to please others — not settling for less than you deserve.

Self-love is:

- Deservingness
You are always worthy.

- Knowing

YOU ARE ENOUGH.

- Self-respect
It's okay to leave the party. Always do what is right for you.

- Gratitude

In every situation (even the not so pretty ones), there is always a lesson to learn and a reason to be grateful for what you have learned and for those around you, starting with yourself.

- Self-control

You are in control of your thoughts, emotions, reactions, and responses.

- Self-care

Take care of your health, mind, body, and soul. You are a beautiful temple; don't fill yourself up with trash!

- Play

Have fun! What did you absolutely love to do as a child? Was it drawing? Was it climbing trees? Maybe it was swimming? Did you read books and love them? How about playing games? Horseback riding? Reconnect with the things you enjoy doing the most.

- Hugs

Family therapist, Virginia Satir said, "We need four hugs a day for survival, eight for maintenance, and 12 for growth." Give more hugs and receive them in return!

- Dreaming

Dreams were placed in your mind and heart for a reason, and they are attainable! Take some time to visualize your dreams. Write them down, make a vision board. Sit outside and enjoy the sunlight and dream your dreams.

- Forgiveness

Forgive yourself and others. Remember, everybody is doing the best they can with the tools they've been given.

- Prayer and Meditation

Stay connected to the One who breathed life into you. Give thanks. Give Love. Sit and be still. Be in awe. Breathe.

- Pride

What are you proud of? Pick something you like about you, then show it off to others! Give yourself a pat on your back.

The more comfortable you become with those things, the more you give permission to others to do the same in their lives -- permission they may not have known they had.

Look at YOU! How great are you, already learning the self-mastery of love!? Learn for yourself and teach others. We feel best when we help others. That is true self-love and empowerment for you and them.

Self-Love Mastery Exercises

Write five things you like about you:

1.

2.

3.

4.

5.

Write five things you could do daily that would make your soul smile:

1.

2.

3.

4.

5.

Who are five people you could call just to give gratitude for being in your life:

1.

2.

3.

4.

5.

What are five lessons you have learned in your past that propelled you into your present greatness:

1.

2.

3.

4.

5.

What are five gratitudes you could write down before you fall asleep tonight:

1.

2.

3.

4.

5.

Here is a short list of some of the things that I have learned to do for me. Things that make me happy. Maybe some or all of these will work for you. Be sure to add your own!

1. Clean your house just for you. Organize your drawers, buy the linens (the good ones!) and use them without having a special occasion — for you!

2. Do not wait until you have guests to light some candles or to use the fancy dishes.

3. Buy the nicest shampoo — for you.

4. Fill your body with proper nutrition, not cheap, toxic food. You are not cheap!

5. Plug in the twinkly lights and enjoy your surroundings. Be present wherever you are.

6. Pat yourself on the back and tell yourself, "You're doing a great job!"

7. Never call yourself or anyone else a bad name.

8. Take a vacation.

9. Surround yourself with the people you love, who love you and ONLY want the best for you.

10. Give yourself grace. This one is important! Remember, the grace you live is the grace you give! To give love freely to others you must first love yourself.

I am not here to inspire. I am here to share me and a part of my life with you, However, if my sharing inspires, then great! There is hope. Remember it's only a story -- a perceived story from my childhood that I've learned on my journey. At any time I can change my perception and change my story. Abandonment? OR Surrender? Loves' greatest sacrifice. I choose Surrender. I choose Love.

self love....Mastery.

Now, go take a bubble bath.

**"We accept the
love we think
we deserve."**

~Stephen Chbosky

CHAPTER SIX

❖

Love: Within

By Marie Crawford

I t's Monday morning, 8:05. I'm zipping in and out of traffic, my heart is beating out of my chest, my anxiety level is rising. Why can't these people get out of my way? Why can't they drive any faster? I keep looking at my phone, anticipating that unwanted berating.

He is such a narcissistic, overbearing tyrant. I know the phone call is coming, just like it does every Monday morning. That loud, unpleasant voice with that unbearable lisp.

Of course I am late, just more ammunition for "The Jerk". That is what everyone secretly calls the general manager.

There it is, as I pull into the parking lot, the call to start my day in the most negative way possible, the conversation that I allow time after time, to immediately change my mindset and my mood. He does all the talking--or should I say shouting-- and I try to barely listen and block it out of mind.

It's just Monday, I think as I hang up the phone. Walking into the building, I check out all the cameras scattered around, inside and outside. Just thinking about how every move and every conversation is monitored. I head straight into the shop and greet the technicians with a good morning and a smile, only to receive scornful looks and complaints about the day's work assignments. I quickly leave that scene and head into the front office. I look at the routes for the day, make any necessary changes, and then go into my office and shut the door.

I have barely been at work an hour and I am already thinking about just running out into traffic as I stare out the window watching vehicles fly by me. I hate working here. I've thought this several times a day and often said it aloud.

.....

I had become very miserable with my team's attitude changes, negative comments, their dread, and lack of motivation since coming to work for The Jerk and his group of drones. I was the manager for a department that I had started up for the company. I had worked with my team for years at another company and we'd left the previous employer to start up a new venture with this company as a team, at my persuasion. I felt so guilty and responsible for everyone's misery. I had convinced people that I had worked with for years, people I cared about-- even my own son, for God's sake--to jump into hell with me. What kind of leader, friend, or mother was I?

I had spent years looking out for these people, protecting their well-being, wading through the trenches with them, only to bring them into this toxic work environment filled with drama and hostility. Every day was consumed by argumentative conversations with The Jerk. There was nobody to talk to about this at the company. The Chief Operating Officer also handled human resources; she was so rude and unpleasant that most people avoided her. She would not even acknowledge people when they spoke to her. I never heard anyone say a nice word about her. This behavior was so pervasive that it was just accepted as the way to carry on day-to-day business. The owner of the company only cared about making money and was very disengaged in the business; he was not concerned about how the employees were treated.

I had been in this industry for fifteen years prior to this venture. I had learned the industry inside and out. I started as a part-time customer service representative and worked my way up to Virginia District Manager, and I'd managed operations and sales for multiple locations. I had built productivity, sincere friendships with the employees, who I considered friends, as well as established relationships with customers, only to hand it all over to The Jerk, who obviously was not holding up his end of the deal.

The Jerk would try to humiliate me publicly. He would call me and put me on speakerphone with other managers in his office to scorn me for mistakes or miscommunication that I was not actually responsible for. Both of The Jerk's lazy, entitled sons were managers as well, so I was often called a liar for something they did or did not do. They would not take responsibility for their incompetence, and he would always take their side. He even told me that he would always believe them over me; I was wasting my breath. I would hang up the phone so angry. How dare he call me a liar! How dare he talk to me in front of my peers like that! How dare I accept this treatment! I remember thinking how much I disliked him.

As my hatred for him grew, so did the hatred for myself. I was focusing on the negativity, drowning myself in alcohol and eating very poorly. Was this the worst decision of my life? Did everyone hate me for leading them down this path and convincing them that this was a good decision? I was allowing this situation to make me miserable and steal my joy.

Divorce

About two years into this job, on March 24, 2016, my husband and I called it quits. This was a very devastating experience for me. We had been together for ten years, five of which we were married. It wasn't a surprise, though; I had known it was coming for about two years. He traveled for work a lot and was struggling with alcoholism. When he was out of town for work, we argued and when he was home, he spent his time with one of his friends drinking or doing an activity he enjoyed. I felt so alone. Not only was he physically unavailable, but he was never emotionally available for me either. Our relationship was filled with extreme highs and lows. I loved this man so much. I loved his smile, the way he dressed, the smell of his cologne, his work ethic, his family… everything I thought I knew about him. We had been through so much together. I had stuck by his side through a drug addiction, disloyal times, lies and so many obstacles, but I never felt like he was there for me.

I could no longer take the emotional roller coaster ride that I was on with him. One minute I was his best friend, his everything, and the next minute I was the worst person he had ever known. He called me names, insulted me, told me I was fat and disgusting and often said he hated me. This was a time in my life when I really needed someone. I felt like I had no escape; I was miserable at work all day and then came home to equal misery. I was in a downward spiral of self-destructive behavior.

Even though I had started working out and had been focused on weight loss for a few months, I was still hanging out with friends who partied all the time; I was staying out late, drinking and not getting enough sleep. I was sad, felt alone and thought about killing myself all the time. I cried myself to sleep a lot. On the outside, I wore a smile for everyone else. I wanted my kids to be happy and not know the pain I was experiencing. I didn't want my friends and family to know how I really felt because I was the rock, the strong one. I was the one who took care of everyone else. I didn't want my coworkers to know the depths of my despair, because there was enough stress at work. I was never good at being vulnerable or letting people know things were not perfect for me.

Our separation was such a surprise to many people because I hadn't shared the struggles and turmoil. I felt better about myself when people saw me as being successful, as having a relationship without problems and having my life together. All I had done was to leave myself feeling alone. It was painful to tell my friends and family what had happened. I felt like a loser. This was my second failed marriage. Between my work situation and my marriage, I thought my world was falling apart. Where was the love I had once had for myself? Where was the care for my well-being? Where was the girl I used to see in the mirror smiling back at me? Where was the courage I had always had?

"We are not what we do, we are not what we have, we are not what others think of us."
- Henri Nouwen

Early Years

You are not your past. That is what I have spent a
lifetime telling myself. But your past does influence so
much of what you feel and your perception of the
world. I grew up in southwest Virginia. My mom was a
waitress and my dad was a coal miner who was so
frequently laid off that he eventually bought a tractor-
trailer and changed careers. I have two sisters. One is
five years older, and the other is one year younger.
Our life was anything but perfect. We lived in a two-
bedroom run-down trailer. The three of us sisters
shared one small bedroom. Money was scarce, and
my parents argued all the time.

My dad was a raging alcoholic who was mentally and
emotionally abusive. I was never the target of his
anger and outrage, but that still didn't make it a less
terrifying experience for a child. He would get drunk,
break things, throw things, flip over the dinner table
with our dinner on it, yell and curse. He was
constantly cursing, belittling and insulting my mom
and my older sister. My dad would often get drunk
and leave to go to who-knows-where. Even as a very
small child, I remember feeling constant worry for his
well-being, even silently crying myself to sleep at
night. I didn't want my mom to see me cry because I

felt like she had enough to worry about at the time. Sometimes I wondered if he would even come back, because he would disappear for weeks at a time, leaving my mom to take care of us and provide. She would always let him come back. I never understood why she endured so much.

Even through this dysfunctional childhood, I never felt unloved by my parents, but I always felt a sense of being trapped in hell with no escape. I was intelligent and excelled in school. Even though I had friends, I often believed nobody really liked me and certainly would care about my hardships, so I never shared very much about my home life.

When I was ten years old, my older sister became really sick. She was in the hospital for some time and then transferred to the University of Virginia Medical Center because her condition was deteriorating. She was soon diagnosed with non-Hodgkin's lymphoma. This cancer originates in the lymphatic system. She was very ill, and it was a serious situation. We were living about 4.5 hours from the University of Virginia, so my parents decided it would be better to move closer to the hospital so that my aunt could help care for my younger sister and me. At the same time, my dad worked and my mom stayed at UVA with my sister.

I will never forget, my dad picked me up from school one day and we were gone the next. It was so scary. I didn't even get to tell my friends goodbye. We eventually started our new school; my sister came home from the hospital. We met new friends and life resumed. My dad was back to the drinking and hell raising before I knew it. Though it sucked, I would escape by playing outside with the neighborhood kids and staying busy. I loved everyone and made the most out of what I had.

The summer before I started eight grade, we moved a couple of miles down the road, too far away to hang out with my friends. It was okay, though. Once eighth grade started, I stayed occupied. I participated in every activity available, anything to avoid being at home. I was so upbeat during the school year that my parents would praise me for loving school and excelling when, in reality, I just didn't want to be at home. I also went to church as often as possible to escape my unbearable home life.

Summers between the ages of thirteen and fourteen were the worst for me. I was overcome by loneliness and felt like I was trapped in that hell. Killing myself was a daily thought. I would cut myself in inconspicuous places so no one would notice. I would plan ways to run away but never followed through. I wasn't depressed; I just didn't see another way to escape.

All of my friends spent their summers hanging out, going places and doing things. Still, by having overprotective parents, I wasn't allowed to go anywhere with my friends and we never had quality time together as a family, not even a vacation together. I just wanted to be out of that house, away from the chaos. I would wake up to screaming, cursing, and arguing almost every day. The house was only two bedrooms and I slept on the couch in the living room. I couldn't even close a door to escape the craziness.

When I was fifteen and a few months old, I was old enough to get a worker's permit. I got my first job. By the time I got my driver's license, I had saved up five hundred dollars to buy my first car. I was back to loving life and myself and felt happiness that I had never felt before. It gave me a whole new sense of self-worth. I felt so free, even though I wasn't really free. I still lived at home, but I went to school all day and got a job and worked every night. By the time I got home from work, my parents were in bed. I loved working. I was making money and could buy myself clothes and shoes that were in style. Up until this point, I was lucky to get one pair of jeans and shoes a year. Frequently, my shoes had holes in them, and if I had a growth spurt, well, you know what those jeans looked like, right?

I was social and had a lot of friends in high school, some older and some my age. I hung out with my older friends mostly and partied with them on the weekends. Most of my friends lived in better houses, drove nicer cars, and wore stylish clothes. I often thought about how lucky their families were and how unlucky my family was. I didn't want my friends to come to my house. I was embarrassed and felt terrible about myself because I didn't even have my own bedroom. On top of that, I was worried my parents would be fighting or arguing, so it was just better to go to other people's houses.

False Hope

I started dating someone when I was sixteen years old, and when I turned eighteen, I decided, even though I was still in high school, I would move out of my parent's house and move in with my boyfriend and his brother. My boyfriend was four years older and I saw him as my savior. He had a good job and apartment. Even though we were completely different and argued all the time, it seemed like a better option then what I had.

After I graduated high school, I attended college. The next year I found out that I was pregnant. Three months after the birth of my son, his father and I got married. Then at twenty-two, I had my daughter. Their father and I stayed together until I was twenty-seven years old. Arguing and drinking had become too much to handle. I felt like I was reliving my childhood, and I refused to allow my children ever to feel the way I had felt. So, we divorced.

I didn't date anyone for about a year after the divorce. Then, I met someone who I thought was wonderful. We dated for about a year and then moved in together. He was great with my children and we got along pretty well. After two years of living together, though, I discovered that he too was an alcoholic. He had been hiding the drinking and lying about going to work. I didn't want someone with an addiction and poor work ethic being my children's role model, so we ended our relationship and he moved out.

Shortly after, I met the person who would be my second husband. It was love at first sight. We had so much fun in the beginning. He traveled for work very often, so when he was home, we would drink and hang out. I thought we partied so much just because we hadn't seen each other in a while. I soon realized this was his lifestyle.

I would do anything for him, though. I was so afraid of losing him if I didn't just go along with whatever he wanted, so I went along with it. He was everything to me. He was handsome and smart. We had good conversations, and he enjoyed traveling. He had a close family, he worked hard, made a good salary, and he liked to have fun. We had so much fun at first. My kids loved him and he loved them.

"Gratitude is the healthiest of all human emotions."

\- Zig Ziglar

I adored his family, and they were so welcoming to my kids and me. But, two years into our relationship, I found out he had an addiction to narcotics. This was a painful discovery. I couldn't believe I had no clue this whole time. But I immediately came to his rescue to help him battle this addiction. It took about two years to get through this struggle, but he did it.

After dating for five years, we got married and I thought everything would be amazing. Then, a couple of years after getting married, I discovered he had only substituted addictions. His drinking had gotten out of control.

When he was out of town working, I could only take his word for what he was doing, but when he was in town, my friends were seeing him leave the liquor store every day and he was lying about it. I was furious, hurt, and sad. I felt so defeated and so low. He was lying to me about drinking, and when I confronted him, we only argued.

Bad turned to worse. I tried drinking with him at first, but it only made me angry because that wasn't what I wanted to do daily. He would drink so much so quickly that he would be passed out early in the evenings and I would be sitting there staring at the walls in our house by myself. If I went out with friends, the next day we would argue because he didn't think I should have gone anywhere. It was a no-win situation.

May 2014, I went to work for The Jerk, and that was about the time I started dealing with the realization that my world was falling apart at home. When my husband and I split up in 2016, I was at what I would consider emotionally the lowest point in my life. As I said, you are not your past. But your past does influence so much of what you feel and your perception of the world and yourself. I was trying to keep a smile and project happiness but was really dying inside.

I had never really focused on my childhood experiences or past relationship experiences until my separation. I had swept those feelings under the rug and filled my life with so many distractions that I didn't have time to think about the things that had hurt me. The breakup from my husband generated a flood of emotions, flashbacks of bad experiences, feelings of defeat and failure, blame and guilt for everything I had ever done wrong or perceived myself to have done wrong. Feelings of unworthiness, shame, and self-doubt hung over my head like a dark cloud.

When I hung out with friends and partied, I felt guilty, like a hypocrite, and I hated myself. When I ate poorly, I felt guilty and hated myself. When I went shopping and spent too much money, I felt guilty and hated myself. I was searching for love and happiness in people and objects but finding nothing but more unfulfilling guilt. I was running from myself, my thoughts, and my feelings. I was reaching and just trying to find love and connection in everyone and everything else besides myself.

Set Free

Friday, April 7, 2017, my desperate pleas for change were finally heard and the universe responded. I had gone to lunch late that day and on my way back to the office, I received a phone call from the customer service representative that The Jerk had sent someone to come and get my laptop. They had told her he was going to fire me and wanted me to go to his office when I returned to work. I called him upon my arrival back to the office and told him that I would prefer he come to my office. I knew what was happening and I was not going to be the last act in his circus.

Upon arrival at my office, The Jerk informed me that my position with the company was being eliminated, effective immediately. I was overcome with joy and excitement. It was shocking; I could not believe this was a happy moment for me! I should have been scared and sad; I was losing my job. I was single and the sole provider; I would have no income. Instead, I felt like a huge burden had been lifted.

> **"Self-worth comes from one thing**
> **- thinking that you are worthy."**
> - Wayne Dyer

Finding Love

Over the next couple of days, I did a lot of reflecting. I decided I was going to take the summer off and use that time to gain clarity about what I was looking for in my life, in a career and a relationship, not just a job for financial stability or any person for the sake of comfort. It was essential to have them both align with my values. I had lost track of setting boundaries, I had abandoned self-care practices, and I had stopped loving myself. Making these commitments to myself-- to not just jump into a job or relationship and settle-- was extremely empowering.

Taking this time was the best decision I could have ever made. The most significant discovery of all for me was that I had never learned to love myself truly. The failed marriages and lousy work experiences were not a reflection of who I was, but rather a reflection of how I felt about myself. Self-doubt, listening to other people's opinions, and not establishing boundaries that reflected my values and expectations had ruled my existence. I had spent a lifetime allowing myself to settle for less than what I wanted and less than what honored my identity. I had focused on what was good for everyone else, but not for me. I had always used distractions and avoidance as coping mechanisms for hard issues rather than facing the problems I had.

When you really pay attention to your pain, you discover so much.

I realized that, to find true love, I would have to look inward to myself, not outward to other people, material objects, or other distractions.

To love myself, I would have to forgive everyone and love everyone. So, that is what I did. I forgave myself for bad decisions, mistakes, and failures. And I forgave everyone who had ever wronged me. People ask how I could just forgive. To me, it was just about being intentional and making a decision to forgive. Letting go of the hurt, bitterness, and anger was exhilarating.

Being appreciative and showing gratitude became an important practice for me. The more I was grateful for, the more I started noticing all the things that I had to be grateful for in life.

"A grateful heart is a magnet for miracles."
-Unknown

I began writing affirmations and posting them everywhere. Loving yourself begins with your thoughts. Your thoughts are the most powerful influences in your life. I read somewhere that even if you don't believe it right now, you should fake it until you make it. It is so true, and, eventually, I started believing these things about myself.

These were and still are essential affirmations for me:

I am enough.

I can release the past and forgive everyone.

The past has no power over me.

I love myself and everyone.

More and more good things are coming to me.

I compare myself only to my higher self.

I live in peace and joy.

"For as he thinketh in his heart, so is he."
- Proverbs 23:7

I began focusing on my health and exercise. At the age of 40, I started running 5Ks and obstacle course races, kickboxing, and became a self-defense instructor to help empower others. I started meeting new friends and, for the first time in my life, I realized the importance of being around like-minded people. It was motivating and encouraging.

I decided that I wasn't going to live in the past. I would let the past be the past. I would remember the lessons learned but let the hurt, pain, resentment, and anger go.

"My mission in life is not merely to survive, but to thrive; and to do so with some passion, some compassion, some humor, and some style."
~ Maya Angelou

After my six-month hiatus, I found a new career with a company that aligned perfectly with my values. I have been at this company for almost three years and it has been a tremendous experience so far. The owner of the company is honest, kind, and understanding. He seeks input, he is appreciative of hard work and dedication, and he hires competent people. My supervisor leads by example. He treats everyone with respect and frequently tells me how much I am appreciated. He is a great mentor and a true inspiration. I have coworkers that I love and consider to be great friends.

I look forward to going to work every day. I have flexibility and a generous amount of paid time off and holidays. I am never micromanaged or criticized. I have been single for four years now, but I know I will meet the right person at the right time. I am thankful that I am more than enough. I am always striving to do better and eager to learn as much as I can. I love with all my heart and I show kindness and compassion to everyone around me.

I am sincerely grateful for the struggles, and I celebrate all the wins. I am just breathing in every moment of this amazing journey. I am perfectly imperfect...a work in progress, but one thing is certain: I have found true love - within myself.

"You cannot be lonely if you like the person you're alone with."
~ Wayne Dyer

"Love is what we are born with.

Fear is what we learn here."

~ Marianne Williamson

CHAPTER SEVEN

❖

Everything is Possible

By Suzanne Rushton

Once upon a time, not so long ago, in an apartment around the corner, I was sitting on my balcony alone. Drinking, smoking, and watching YouTube videos for the thousandth time, I looked around and asked the universe if this was happiness. As in, if I lived every day for the rest of my life the way I did today, would this be enough?

Of course, I knew the answer.

It was around that time that I could no longer deny the smoldering awareness of the hole I was digging for myself. I wondered how deep the hole was and if it was too late to escape. It was a familiar hole—I knew it was there—but I seemed to keep winding up in it.

It became increasingly clear that things had to change. A lot. Drastic, dramatic action was required!

But what does that even mean? Where do you start when everything needs to change?

I was living in a cave. Physically it was a bright, new apartment in Vancouver, but emotionally it was a void. A dimly lit, emotional, physical, and spiritual black hole. I refer to this period as "the dark ages" both to be dramatic and to be honest, because I was completely uninspired, demotivated, and directionless. I tried to stay productive in the cave, and I'd like to say that I was, but I really wasn't. Not in any meaningful way. Unless you count treading water as being productive.

What's more, this went far beyond un-productivity. I was making downright questionable choices about my health. Explaining or hiding this from people (and myself) became exhausting, so staying home became easier.

In addition to the health situation, I noticed that my business was stalling— not declining, just not accelerating. And, worse, I didn't care. I've always felt capable of doing great things but, instead, I was spending every night at home alone on the balcony. I had no interest in developing...anything. People would invite me to things and I'd either decline or say maybe and then not go. I had painted myself into the smallest corner. I started wallowing deeper and deeper, and the negative thought patterns became more and more solidified.

My body and brain started to believe that this was the new normal. Kind of like, *well, this is my life now. You aren't in shape, you don't eat well, you don't take care of yourself, you can't accomplish your goals, you're unattractive, people don't like the real you, you have fatal flaws and will never be able to find a partner*...on and on. Thanks, brain. I lost my sex drive altogether. I couldn't remember the last time I was excited at the idea of being with a man, and, no, I didn't switch teams. If this sounds like a mind-numbing story to you, you would be correct.

I was managing-ish, so I could pretend I was sort of okay. But I knew the truth. I had a feeling that I was capable of so much more. But my turning point came when I started thinking that maybe I wasn't. Perhaps I *wasn't* capable of more. I started believing my own bullshit. And it was painful.

It became clear that I was in an abusive relationship with myself and had been for quite some time.

As the saying goes, we change when the pain of staying the same outweighs the pain of change. And so, I had to change. I didn't know how specifically, but I did know who, when, what, and why. Me, now, and everything...because I was broken.

I took some wrong turns and had some false starts. The first one was a trip to the doctor. On the face of it, I made the appointment because I had a sore throat that would not go away. (You would think I would have quit smoking during that time, but I did not.) The receptionist had me fill out some forms about depression and anxiety, which was my first clue that this visit wasn't about my throat.

I remember feeling vaguely hopeful that maybe there was something that could be done about my state of mind (or my throat). As it turned out, I had used antidepressants in the distant past, so the doctor wanted to see how I was doing now. I told him I wasn't doing well, but I was still showering, working, and brushing my teeth. So, I guess that made me not quite depressed enough to qualify for medication. I cried on the way back to the car and in the car afterward for a while. I had come so close to having help or a solution and it had slipped away. Later I wondered if I should have lied about the state of affairs. How far off from normal *was* I? I felt destitute. And my throat was still sore.

I'll summarize a few of the other things I did that were part of the journey, but not worth going into in any depth right now.

I went to a workshop and did a Wheel of Life exercise, by which I identified that, basically, the only thing going well in my life up to that point was finances. Good to have that one, I suppose, the benefits of hiding behind work, but that did leave seven other areas of life that were lacking. Yowzers! But not a shock to anyone.

I hired a life coach. I needed help with accountability, and I needed a manager since, at that time, I wasn't capable of self-managing. I can't say she was the best fit, but she helped me get focused.

I remember thinking that because I was so utterly incapable of doing anything helpful for myself, I would enlist the help of all the people to get me back on track until I could do things myself. Although it came from a place of weakness, the idea was solid. I started going to a naturopath, and I ordered food from meal provider websites. (Yes, I was too lazy to buy food and cook it.) I hired a personal trainer to come to my apartment gym since mental health is directly linked to physical health and I was not getting any stronger, more flexible, or graceful sitting on the balcony. I enrolled in an aerial silks class at a circus school. I didn't do very well, but I emerged with a desire to strengthen my upper body. Yay, a goal! Goals had become scarce.

All of these things helped, and I started making progress. But the river I was flowing down took me in another direction—one with a twist. (WHAT IS THE TWIST?)

Somewhere along the way, I signed up for a contact improv workshop and *loved it*! I loved the feeling of connection, from the ground, from the people, from the space. It's a body awareness exercise, and that unlocked a massive key for me: awareness. It took place at a dance studio, a beautiful open space with lovely, open-minded people. It made me fall in love with movement and for a brief moment, I didn't feel bad about myself. This was the first brick in a foundation that has become central to my life, and it opened the door to a hallway of opportunity that I always suspected was there but really had to seek out to find. It was like an advanced level of a video game that requires a specific sequence of activities to unlock.

I'd been doing a sort of regular but informal mastermind with a friend. He happened to mention he was going to a breath workshop. I'd never heard of these before, but I wasted no time inviting myself. I'm not sure what the pull was, but it was magnetic. Perhaps I knew as a smoker I had lung stuff going on and hoped that breathing would help breathe awareness into the area, pun absolutely intended.

We performed a cacao ceremony before the workshop, which, as I have come to learn, facilitates heart-opening. We set intentions before breathing. And, well, wow. I have never felt so much in such a short period ever in my life. I had physical sensations and hallucinations of all kinds, temperature fluctuations, mind expansions, deep revelations, and a lot more! I have now come to realize that this is normal for a breath workshop.

Things started rapidly picking up pace around this time. A few days after the first breath workshop, I was introduced to a woman who does guided psilocybin journeys. Shortly after that, I went for a biofeedback session with a client who had been teasing me with this for years. Do you know what it said I needed to work on above all else? Heart opening. Not depression, breathing, adrenal fatigue, or some mineral deficiency, but heart-opening.

Ohhh-kay. Okay.

Well, there it began. Heart-opening was my new goal. It still is. It makes total sense when I think about it. I hadn't been interested in dating anyone for so long; my heart had retreated into a tiny cave with no light and was scared to see the light of day. If I stayed in the back of the cave, then I was safe, right? The problem is, it's attached to the rest of me, and I wasn't living the rest of my life either. I was just huddled in the back of my small, dark cave waiting out my days, wondering how many there would be, and escaping every single moment. So yeah, heart opening made huge sense.

Now I had a goal. And a small spring of hope! There was beauty in the simplicity of it all. It turns out I crave simplicity. Gone were all the thoughts of "I should make this much money per month," "I should buy a tiny house," "I should work out more." All the shoulding on myself. The shoulds didn't disappear completely, but heart-opening became my main focus. That was all. That still is all. All other goals pale in comparison. You may be noticing a pattern. I was after a complete paradigm shift and was willing to do anything and everything to get it.

At my second breath workshop, I initially felt awkward, like I wasn't doing it properly. I got over myself and went inwards, and amazingly, I was able to look into my heart and see that what the world needs is for me to discover myself truly. In awakening myself, I will be able to help awaken others. There's something powerful and freeing about being around someone who has found themselves. When you encounter such a person, you feel safe to be yourself, too. And that is my goal, to be and offer that safe space to others.

At that moment, I saw it clearly: my experience can help awaken others. My perception of what other people think is utterly useless and all I need to do is have my experience and live my life, and the rest will fall into place. That is how I can be of the most service to the world, to myself and others. What a revelation!

As the session drew to an end, I felt sad at the loss of love and sad that it was ending, even though I had known it was going to go away. I battled within. I had ALL the insights and ALL the emotions. My heart was touched, my entire system moved, and now, in hindsight, I realized that I was being opened, or allowing myself to be opened, as was my intention. I was able to let go. Not entirely, but I felt stirrings, and it was such a beautiful, incredible and powerful experience. I felt like I didn't need all of the things I've always felt sorry for myself for not having, or things I'd been seeking. I realized that *I am* supported in all the ways I need. I felt beautiful and lovable and worthy, and all the things that I'd lost sight of in recent years.

Sometimes I think that my world works in giant karmic waves. I've had periods in my life filled with abundance and companionship, and, conversely, there have been great voids. The tide goes in; the tide goes out. Discovering breathwork was when I felt the tide start on its way back in, this cycle bringing something new and fundamental with it. An awakening.

Finally, in November, I went on my guided psilocybin journey. I won't go into detail, but the takeaways were all in line with my heart-opening goal. It's okay to rely on a power higher than myself to invoke change. Twelve-step programs exist because people need a power greater than themselves. This suddenly made so much sense. I'd always felt terrible that I wasn't motivated to take care of myself, for myself. Like, why not? What's wrong with me? Everyone else seems to have this figured out. But, as it turns out, I don't have to do it alone. I found this immensely reassuring.

The trip also drove home the idea that the cave is a form of rebirth—a cocoon. Things need to die before they are reborn. Conception was a big theme that day. Some flowers take many years to bloom, sometimes decades, and we're not all the same. It's okay to need hibernation or incubation time.

Looking back, I think I was just tired. Tired of all the energy output, living in the city, running in circles, climbing ladders without knowing where they lead. With the help of my guide, we reframed my existence. Not bad for a day's work.

I feel extreme gratitude for the journey and my guide. She was like the sister I never had. She held me and laughed and cried with me for the entire day. I recommend this for everyone.

Following the journey, things went into overdrive. I started to say, write, and believe, "anything is possible." This became my new mantra. Saying is believing (when it comes to me, anyway). I took every should that I had and turned it into an "it is possible" statement. It's possible to…go for a run, build a tiny house, save x amount of dollars, eat vegetables, etc. Everything is possible. I don't even have to do anything; all I need to do is believe it's possible! It is possible to be vibrant, to feel loved, to love, to feel energetic. You get the idea; the list is long! I took action steps towards removing a toxic business partner from my life, an issue that I'd previously been unsure how to address. I quit drinking altogether. I hired another personal trainer who was a better fit. I found and hired a superstar employee to help with a stagnant business and managed to attract someone who is passionate and talented. Things started moving quickly. In short, my vibration was raised. (I know this is a book, but please imagine a bunch of heart emojis here like an Instagram live video.)

Christmas came and went without a hitch. I enjoyed the time I spent with my parents. I managed to avoid being triggered by my dad, and my mom commented that I seemed more present. I was practicing compassionate listening learned from Thich Nhat Han. I started reading *Getting Things Done*, by David Allen, which is basically the book I've been searching for my entire life. I lust after organization. It's on every to-do list I've ever made. I get aroused by highly organized people and have huge inferiority complexes around them. This book is the key to it all.

So, THAT was exciting. I read it thoroughly, with passion, and started implementing it right away! It's a work in progress, but I really feel like I'm on the path. It is possible to be organized.

I started going to a local pole dancing studio like I've wanted to for years. I had always told myself there was no point going because I didn't have a pole at home and no way to practice. But I decided, fuck it. I'll just go because I love being there. My theory is, if I do what makes me happy today, in five years I'll have a bunch of days to look back on in which I was delighted!

I came across some wisdom which says, "if you are worrying about your purpose, then you do not truly love what you are doing. Your purpose will always reveal itself in the end, through the amazing diversity of your experiences." So, my goal, to open my heart, believe everything is possible, and live fully today, is all I need to focus on.

The sun was starting to come out. Things that previously seemed insurmountable became possible. I quit smoking. I figured I could always lose weight later, but the most addictive things had to go first. It had become possible for me to stop and, lo and behold, it happened. I went to a writing meetup group. I love writing and have always been a writer (or recorder, or capturer of sorts) but haven't done anything personal for ages. I went, and—wouldn't you know it—only days afterward, I was asked to contribute to a book. This book. I had to say yes. For so many reasons, one of which being that I do well with deadlines. I'm not so amazing at accomplishing things for myself, but I'm pretty great at accomplishing things for others!

All of these things started flowing into my life because of focusing on opening my heart in all that I do. I think I've been scared to open my heart because I'm terrified to be myself—the idea of being pure is something I find liberating but still scary.

Opening my heart has led to a shift in mindset. I have always seen myself as a solo warrior and have been crippled by an overwhelming feeling of being alone and of having to do everything myself—of having no support. I was tired of working so much all the time just to survive. But I now know that I am not alone. It's okay to enter into the rest and repair phase and trust that things will work out as they're meant to. It is possible to feel supported, abundant, and feel like the universe is a safe place.

You can see my old mindset in how I thought about partnership: I can't meet anyone because I'm too busy working. I have to work double as much as everyone else who has a partner because I'm paying full rent myself and I'm self-employed, and so on. It's a vicious circle. I've never been hungry or homeless, but yet I kept myself trapped in this cycle of saying yes to all the work because of a scarcity mindset but also from fear of being vulnerable to someone.

You can see my new mindset in the trust I am building with myself. I am the most valuable relationship I will ever have. I'm getting healthier by turning pro with my health and starting to bloom. I'm paying attention to the thoughts and stories I tell myself. Identifying destructive thought patterns has been helpful. I think I've had a case of overwhelming opposition to living my life, which has held me back in all sorts of ways. I see now that resistance points towards what most needs shifting.

I am happy to say that I am now pointed in the right direction. And just like you don't work out once and get in shape, I have implemented a spiritual workout regime that supports my growth and overall wellbeing.

At the end of the day, the things that make me happiest are movement, fresh air, expression, and connection. I am now pursuing those things at the cost of all other things and trusting that, if you genuinely love what you are doing, your purpose will always reveal itself in the end. So, be happy now, whatever it takes. Do you know how relieving that is? I've spent *so much time* worrying about what my long-term plans are and if I'm getting any closer to them!

It is possible to feel inspired, invigorated, energetic, and healthy.

Here are my top three takeaways for anyone who feels stuck but dreams of living a fuck-yes life:

1. Don't give up wondering if this is it. It's not! If you think there is another life waiting for you, you are correct. The cave is an incubation period and doesn't need to be permanent. The world is friendly and people want to be helpful. Reach out for help and don't stop reaching. Ever.

2. Breath workshops are doorways to awareness and heart-opening. They are super-useful tools you can use to stimulate a paradigm shift. Yes

I'm biased, but I highly encourage you to give one a try.

3. Forget about long-term goals and make yourself happy today. Keep it that simple. By creating happiness today, the rest will fall into place. I guarantee it. As Steve Jobs says, the dots always connect at the end.

My path to self-love has not been direct, and I don't anticipate it being direct from here on either. I wouldn't want it to be any other way, as counter-intuitive as that may seem, I have discovered the joy in not knowing how my life is going to play out. That feels good to me. I'm grateful to know there is a path and that I'm on it, and there are people to help me return to it when I'm lost.

Ultimately, the cave is part of the path, and within the cave are lessons. If gold were easy to find, it wouldn't be as valuable.

"To love is to return to a home that we never left, to remember who we are."

~ Sam Keen

CHAPTER EIGHT

❖

Love Wins in the End

By Ryan Doherty

The most magnificent love affair of my life has been with my partner in growth, Jen, and my three-year-old son, Ethan, who never ceases to amaze me. What joy, peace, love, and transcendence I feel from being in an awakened state every time I "fire and wire." I can actually feel my body creating and strengthening new neurological pathways from experiences which install beliefs beyond what was previously evidenced as possible.

These new feelings shook my old, conditioned, unconscious patterns, and they are truly enlightening. Witnessing the birth of our baby boy and taking annual holiday trips to the Philippines to visit and take Jen's extended family to destinations like Baguio, Buang, or Boracay...these are the moments to open the heart and reminisce about.

One of our many Philippines adventures included me driving from Angeles City, 80kms north of Manila, tackling and negotiating the meandering congestive traffic of Manila whilst driving on the opposite side of the road from what I was accustomed to, only to go south to Villa Escudero Plantation and Resort to attend a friend's wedding. Our party included nine adults and three kids under three. As if the drive were not exciting enough, the whole group of us also enjoyed a ride on a caribou-led cart while being serenaded by some local musicians, allowing us to experience the traditions of yesteryear. What you focus on expands, so what could be more important than focusing on the positive aspects of my closest family relationships?

My first 30 years were largely spent repeating patterns that were given to me by past generations, and those patterns did not serve me well. This resulted in responses of hurt and jealousy, comparisons of self with others, and resentment within the family unit. I wasn't aware of the costs that I would pay for following the thoughts and feelings that made me shy away from the world every time life got a little hard to bear. I found myself very limited in my ability to love and be loved.

Looking back now, I can see that my limiting beliefs stemmed from how my dad grew up and his parents before him. My dad's parents were both hard-working and both had their own histories of negatively anchored lives. My dad said that he could never please his father, and I used to hear the statement of "you will never win an argument with me" that his father had said to him, which seemed to cut my dad deeply.

My grandmother was born in Edinburgh, Scotland, and the story goes that her own father, a brilliant engineer, had concocted a chemical cocktail that would take himself and his only daughter out of this world, as he did not want to lose his precious daughter to marriage with my grandfather. My grandmother, who I only saw but a handful of times in my life, drank a flagon of sherry well into her 90s, a habit she began after my grandfather had passed away in his sleep at the age of 82. My grandma was tough in nature, diminutive at 4 feet, 8 and a half inches—and she would remind you to not forget the half inch! My dad grew up thinking he was not loved because his mother was hard on him, as was common back then.

Even though my dad was the second youngest boilermaker the year he went through his apprenticeship in Victoria, he didn't seem to have much respect for his own father. My dad lived through a lifetime of his father's jealousy, which seemed to stem from his own childhood trauma.

Having not grown up where love was easily expressed, it wasn't until I took a personal development course through Landmark, for the purpose of breaking my own habitual cycles and letting go of family trauma, that I discovered a true awareness of love, attracted the love of my life, and went on to create a family from love.

Your Past Does Not Define You

I was born in 1976 in a Queensland country town, which was 80kms from where I would live and grow up for the next 17 years of my life. When I was only one, my parents divorced, and my dad, a coal miner, fought and won custody of me. Back then, being orphaned wasn't uncommon, so I feel blessed for the life my dad provided for me. He had many homemakers come and go until Frankie, my guardian mother, arrived and raised me like her own child as best as she could. Although the home I grew up in was safe and secure, I still had ingrained beliefs of not being good enough and of being unworthy of love.

At the age of two, I nearly drowned, which left me with a fear of water for much of my childhood. I remember receiving a D for swimming on my school report card in Grade 1—my first and only failure in primary school. I vividly recall Frankie's signature on my report cards and permission slips, and I got it in my head that having a guardian parent and not a real mom in my life meant that my birth mother did not love me.

My birth mother lived in Melbourne — 2000kms from where I lived — and had started a new family with two daughters who were much younger. Now, I know my dad well enough to be sure that lying is against his nature, but his beliefs about his experiences do not always make them the truth. When trying to tell me about my mother, he said that she may have had schizophrenia. My dad retold the story many a time about how he took my mother to a psychologist to find out why she had high highs and low lows and always joked about how she managed to turn the wheels around and convince the psychologist that it was my dad who had a problem.

So, in believing my dad from a young age, I started to think that there was something wrong with me, because at times when you are in a lower frequency of vibration, you tend to perpetuate thoughts aligned with those feelings, which then become anchored by poor decisions you've made for yourself. Keep in mind that back in the 1970s there was no internet, no way of knowing if there was a mental health issue with my mother or perhaps me. Schizophrenia existed and was talked about. Maybe it was bi-polar, or maybe it was nothing at all, but whatever the case, it made me think negatively about myself as I got older.

Despite these thoughts arising in my mind from time to time, I did go on and do well at primary school, and one proud success I had as a child was attaining a black belt in karate by the age of twelve and being awarded "Peewee of the Year" in our little dojo.

For most teenagers, how you navigate through high school can make or break your path in life. I was no different. I started liking girls in the first year, and experiencing rejection, which shattered my already fragile psyche. I developed a self-conscious disposition because of deepening freckles, and I always found a way to hide out and avoid people when I felt the uncomfortable feelings rising up. I didn't know how to express my feelings to my father, and I felt trapped by what others thought of me.

I tried to find social acceptance by hanging out with a guy who didn't get the best grades but had a reputation as one of the cool kids. He was funny, had the gift of gab, and lived close to me, so it was easy to spend time together after school. We would get in trouble with the police for an incident and I was never considered a ringleader, just the innocent party going along with the crowd and trying to fit in. Over time, my grades dropped dramatically, and I went from topping all my subjects and being the polite and diligent student at school to failing several classes. My dad let me know of his disappointment in my school grades, as he knew I could do better. As the only son and only child, I sunk into a kind of depression at the prospect of losing love from my father — the only male I looked up to in life.

Whenever I thought about getting a part-time job while still at school, I felt too shy to ask around. It seemed like every other week other kids were landing jobs as a shelf-stocker at the local supermarket, as a newsagent, or as a clerk at the video shop. I also became embarrassed by my parents, especially my dad as he was short and balding with glasses and false teeth, and my shallow perception of how one must look became an extension of my shyness complex. I wanted to become handsome, wealthy, and popular in life. I wanted to be valued, and so I embodied these shallow traits that led me to put attractive, successful, much loved persons on a pedestal and therefore consequently put myself in the pit.

The usual embarrassment that kids naturally feel about their parents caused me to keep my parents from attending any school functions, whether it was a school play or awards night. My dad didn't push me to get a job, but, as I had no other ambition, I decided to study hard at school to avoid the weight of any further criticism by myself or from others. I did turn my grades around in years 11 and 12 to finish with an entry into a bachelor's degree program in mechanical engineering in Brisbane. But when the last day of school came, I felt completely lost because I was about to leave the place where I had felt the most certainty in my life.

The School of Hard Knocks

In my first year of university, I developed homesickness after leaving the small town I grew up in and moving to the big city of Brisbane. After only one year, I was kicked out of the engineering program because of my low GPA, so I decided to drop out of university and move back home. I tried again in another town a little closer to home and did the same, this time dropping out of university for good. I picked up jobs like pizza deliverer, cream packer, and working with Australia Post parcel service to pay for my living expenses.

With another two years of life experiences under my belt and more heartache stories, I returned home for an extended period. Within a few months, I hit upon an electrical apprenticeship with the state government, so I moved back to Brisbane. I was living in a boarding house in East Brisbane, a rundown house of about ten rooms. My rent was $40 per week. At age 22, I was by far the youngest person in this place, and most tenants were unemployed, on drugs, or in and out of jail. But I was lucky to have some people there who looked out for me to make sure I was safe. The advantage of being in this place was that it allowed me to save thousands of dollars while I worked as much as I could doing overtime on the weekends and living the simple life.

At the end of the first year of my apprenticeship to become an electrician, I proudly took holidays. Leaving behind that boarding house with all my belongings in a suitcase, I visited my real mum and half-sisters, Kate and Abbie, in Melbourne for our first official time together since I was about eight. I remember eating pizza at Smoking Joe's and wanting to impress my sisters and their boyfriends by eating the most amount of pizza and pasta because, being the older male, I felt I should be the strongest. Although I acted normal with the younger folks and even showed off a little, I remember acting shy and reserved towards my mother. I wanted to meet my half-sisters, but, unfortunately for my birth mother, I felt a blockage to being close to her, a feeling that I had not expected.

Within a day of leaving Melbourne, I arrived back in my home town to see my dad and Frankie. This was the first time in my life that I'd felt secure in a job, and we caught up with each other over the barbeque, and I did the cooking, a role I've enjoyed since I first held a cooking spatula at age ten. We shared many of our favorite dishes, especially seared thinly sliced real potato dipped in tomato sauce, cooked crispy enough to enjoy the cooked taste but with enough tenderness to taste the potato center.

When I arrived back in Brisbane for the second year of my apprenticeship, I decided to move to a more upmarket boarding house, which brought my rent up from $40 a week to about $90, and I was hoping for better boarders. Yet, I was befriended by a con man named Stewart. I met him at a time in his life when he was on the run from the police. A smooth-talking former car salesman, Stewart managed to convince me to join him in a car brokerage business in which he would source cars and on-sell to prospective customers.

Young, naïve, and wanting a better life, I took the opportunity to supplement my low electrical apprenticeship wage. I was doing a three-month stint at police headquarters as part of my electrical training when I found out that Stewart had flown the coop. He had paid for a Mercedes Benz with a cheque that bounced. I was afraid the police might suspect me as an accomplice; however, they assured me that I was only a victim in this matter. Stewart had convinced me to buy a cheap car for us to get around and also to pay for his rent until he skipped town. I had spent most of my savings and felt devastated for allowing someone to trick me. I moved into a place on my own, where I stayed for the next five years to ensure that something like this this would not happen again.

During this time, I developed chronic, nearly debilitating back pain in my lower thoracic L4, L5. It reached the point where I wanted to quit my apprenticeship and quit life. I had seen a psychologist who, at this time in my life, didn't help me with his opinions about my mental outlook. I look back now and know he was right about the stories I told myself and how I painted a picture of a broken human mind, but he did not offer me any hope in any way. In fact, he furthered my downward spiral.

WorkCover Queensland came through, for my injury was a result, in part, from lifting heavy government furniture as part of my work duties. I was put on light duties, no lifting over 10kgs. WorkCover reimbursed me for chiropractic, physiotherapy, and acupuncture sessions, as well as cortisone injections to numb the pain, all of which had failed to help. The flexibility and normal range in my spinal movement could not explain the excruciating pain that was present. I was starting to think that the pain was all in my mind, as I could not separate my negative swirling thoughts from the intense physical pain. Surgery was offered, which had its own percentage of failure that could lead to permanent disability.

Then, Y2K happened — a new millennium, when most people consciously made new resolutions to join a gym and exercise. As a last resort to cure the pain, WorkCover enrolled me in a $70 per month membership to a gym in Stafford. The gym was above a noisy skating rink with one walkway up the middle and gym equipment on both sides of the sidewalk.

When I started to work out, I weighed in at 69.5kg. Now, despite the excruciating daily back pain, it seemed that weight training had shifted my focus away from it. Within a year, I added 10kgs of muscle to my lean frame, building the weak muscles around the problem area in my vertebrae, and a new confidence within me was emerging. I do not even remember when the pain in my back disappeared; I just knew I had become addicted (or maybe obsessed!) with working out. What started with a workout plan and a measurement scorecard to keep track of my progress became a declaration of discipline that was evident in my new physique.

Eighteen months after I started working out, I placed third in my first bodybuilding competition in under 75kg. Because ANB (Australian Natural Bodybuilding) offered the under 75kg weight category for the Queensland competition and I placed, I was lucky enough to then qualify and compete at the national level in under 80kg category. Unlike in high school when I would be called skinny for sucking my stomach in after walking out of the change rooms at the local swimming pool, I now proudly sported six-pack abs in my forties.

The following years presented more challenges to self-love and acceptance. I had started an electrical apprenticeship with the eagerness and intention of becoming a fully licensed electrician, but unfortunately, with my lack of training, I wasn't able to achieve my license and didn't know what to do next. I realized that I was not confident enough to work as an electrician and this presented another blow to my outlook on life.

Before I could stop, break the emotional cycle, and assess my situation for a change in perspective, I reverted back to my old ways of self-destruction. I started doing various sales and marketing jobs, using the confidence from my physique to make it seem like I had it together. Before I knew it, I found myself leaving my professional career, just wanting to have fun and experience life, so I teamed up with my best friend and burned the party candle at both ends. He had come from a traumatic childhood and we both shared in wanting to have a cool facade to hide the hurt little boys inside us.

For six months, we frequented music festivals, nightclubs, raves, and day clubs (clubs that opened at 5 a.m. and were for the hardcore revelers). I worked, gymed it up, and partied around the clock until something happened that caused my life to flash before me.

On a cold winter night following the day I quit a high-end sales job, I partied too hard with alcohol and regretfully took to the steering wheel of my car. After coming off the highway to a service road approaching a roundabout, I carelessly drove my car into the cavernous ditch on the inner rim of the roundabout, plunging six meters with such a force that my hands bent the steering wheel and popped the windscreen out, permanently damaging the car. I was lucky that a previous rain had created mud which brought the car to a halt.

This was a stark reminder of how precious life is. My near death experience from drinking and driving caused me to never go back to my wild ways again. So, with the support from the government, I went back and finished my electrical trade and spent six months in practical training, ensuring that I became fully qualified. I then went on to secure a long-term electrical maintenance role with an electrical contractor to the Queensland Department of Housing. With all that had happened to me, I came to the realization that the universe was working for me and these are the lessons I had to learn before I could become who I wanted to be.

Three years after I drove my car into the ditch, I felt it was time to buy another car, raise my standards, and live a different type of life than the one I had been living. At first, I found a vehicle on the internet, a 1998 Volkswagen Passat with a 2.8L Vr6 motor, eight-speaker stereo, wood grain accents, and wood grain lever five-speed Tiptronic gearbox. It felt like a law of attraction kind of thing, when after two months of seeing this car on the net, I took it from the showroom to the street. I did not want the usual tradesman ute; I wanted a vehicle to represent the kind of person I wanted to become: confident and classy.

In the same week of buying my new ride, I started modern jive dancing at a hall in Spring Hill. There was a mixed group of ladies and gentlemen, and there was a beginner class, followed by intermediate levels, with freestyle dancing in between. Each night, we would learn the basic short routine of a couple of moves, and the females were rotated through the males every step of the way. When it came to freestyle time, the round in which we were supposed to ask someone for a dance, I spent the first couple of months hiding out in my car due to my lingering lack of confidence. Eventually, however, I became confident enough to take girls for a swing.

The dance company offered courses in routines, and I started learning sequences to advance my skills. To replace my old habits of raves, nightclubs, and partying, I began to dance seven days a week in different modalities and enjoyed the occasional Latin and ballroom circuits.

Life was becoming filled with rich activity. Then, in April, my world stopped again. My best friend from the past, whom I had not seen for months, took his own life. He was 32 years old. I wish I could have been there for him, but I, too, was still unconscious and unaware of how a complete change in perspective can alter your destiny in life. But I kept dancing, and later in the year at Modern Jive Nationals, I took third place with a dance partner in the beginner's division.

Landmark, Loving Life, and Finding Love

The Landmark Forum is a three-day personal development course that I truly believed changed my life. It is the introductory course from Landmark Education and is set in a seminar environment with between 100 and 200 participants. People enrol from word-of-mouth conversations with people they know who have had breakthroughs or gained benefit from the course. The Landmark Forum is held in 125 cities in 23 countries and to date has had over 2.2 million participants.

The idea to go to the Landmark Forum came from a conversation I had with a complete stranger whom I met at my local gym. I was inspired by what he said. He was talking about how this program changes your outlook in life and said it could help me with building confidence. You get to complete your past and generate a new way of being. I was intrigued.

For the month of July 2007, I planned a three-week holiday to Melbourne to compete as an intermediate dancer, and I enrolled into the Landmark Forum, as the dates fell perfectly around my birthday, which was one week before the dance competition.

The day of the forum arrived, and I excitedly entered the foyer, picked up a name badge from the smiling volunteer assistants, and went into the seminar room. It was filled with perfectly aligned chairs for about 200 participants. The room was purposely void of visual distraction and set the scene for maximum immersion: maximum immersion by way of listening to the conversations and focusing on being present. The days were long, finishing late into the evening; however, I was okay with this because it was the result I had come for and I had no desire to give anymore resistance to the inherent flow of life.

At exactly 9:00 a.m., as a sign of integrity, our Landmark Forum leader, Cathy Elliot, made her way to the front of the room, dressed sharply in grey business attire with full-length pleated pants and displaying a fit physique chiseled from years of equestrian competition. I sensed the place immediately warm to her divinity-like presence, and I think my subconscious mind related to how closely she resembled my kind-hearted guardian mother, Frankie. Cathy led the proceedings with perfectly articulated wisdom and conscious use of language. For each point she made, a participant would share a story that had a hold on his or her thinking and therefore the quality of his/her own life. She would coach the whole room to a higher state of awareness to see, not only the supposed problem, but how a perspective from a different vantage point, often distinguished in language, can shift the weight of the problem, dissolving incomplete stories and opening the space for new and empowering contexts.

On the first day, one of the actions I made from being in the program was to call my mom, and on a separate call, my dad, to acknowledge them for being the source of my life and to tell them that I love them and that without them I would not exist. Both of my parents may have known that I loved them, but this was the first time I was present and taking responsibility for how my life was turning out rather than being fixed in rigid complaint and shifting the blame from me to an external subject, chiefly my parents. They were each humbled by the experience, and I connected with each of them at a deeper human level.

That night, I started to feel the effects of anchoring the new empowering beliefs I'd gained from the little wins I'd made that day, overcoming fears I had from the past.

Sunday afternoon revealed the ultimate transformation and culminated in a discovery borne from three days of listening, participating in the syllabus content, and hearing the many stories of our lives. Without giving too much away, from my viewpoint, this experience brought the realization that all meaning in our lives is context-dependent, that life is empty and meaningless until you give it meaning.

What I believe happened for me is, my brain realized that all of my stories, whether true or not, do not need to mean anything, and my holding onto a perceptual position of some events that had happened in my life was to keep me disempowered because of a fear of having similar occurrences to continue in my life, a kind of foreboding of repeating previous experiences. Simply put, this felt like the closest to spiritual enlightenment I could imagine, whereby the incessant monkey chatter that is our repetitive thoughts and conversations of the mind all fell silent, thereby removing the negatively bound energy. I would later read and hear of similar experiences from people in the new age space, people like Eckhardt Tolle and Esther Hicks, who use terminology like "nothingness" and "into the vortex." All I know is, it delivered me peace, a depth of life where I could hear more clearly and see colors more vividly.

I like using the analogy of cleaning up the trash files or removing viruses from a slow computer to make it run efficiently again. It made me return to the love that always permeates every divine experience, a love that existed before my conception. For, when you are in your natural state of being, free from fear, complaint, and negative emotions, you can see the oneness of it all; you can feel the love of all sentient beings.

The day of the dance competition arrived and marked the happiest day of my life up until now. I invited my biological mom, Elaine, and half-sisters, Kate and Abbie to breakfast, and we sat at a long table that overlooked the event and stage below. Following the course I was feeling the closest I had ever been to my mom and knew that she was proud of my new direction and attitude towards life.

The competition venue was Federation Square, which has full-length large bay windows that allow people from downtown Melbourne to see inside from the street as dancers highlight their moves to the delight of the crowds. The moment came for me to enter the competition. I was wearing a tailored, tightly fitting white Latin ballroom costume, black dance pants and black suede dancing shoes. With my new brimming confidence, I breathed in the electrically charged air as the exciting moment mounted to my name being announced. As my name rang out, I unleashed three quick spins and hit the dance floor.

As the music began to play, I soon realized how everything was moving in slow motion. The dance category was called "Dance with a Stranger," and you could have a conversation with the competitor girls as you danced with them until the announcer ushered them around to the next gentleman. This event allows you to display your skills with a new partner you may have never met or danced with before, showcasing your adaptability. Like time standing still, I was not trying to be anywhere else, and I enjoyed every moment of being distinct from the boy who grew up so shy and desperately needing to be loved.

I didn't go on to place in the competition, but for once in my life, winning wasn't everything. I congratulated my fellow dancers who surprised themselves by winning places, and I found new importance in just enjoying the scenery of people as a whole.

The competition was early in the day, culminating with a dance party event in the evening to unwind and make new friends with competitors from all around Australia. A cool thing happened when the music started playing and no one, not even the best dancers, took to the floor. I had gotten out of my costume and changed into a more relaxed Kenneth Cole black and green pinstripe silk shirt, dance pants, and my favorite Hugo Boss leather shoes — the kind that make a booming sound when you slam the timber with your heels. I took a girl from the audience for a dance and the room completely stopped to watch us. Then, one by one, the other dancers starting partnering off and came down to the floor and relaxed into what they enjoyed most, the expression of themselves in dance.

Because of the empowerment in transformation that I experienced from the Landmark Forum, I immediately registered and flew back to Melbourne to take the advanced course with Cathy Elliot. While the forum gets you back to nothingness, completing the past and experiencing *being,* the advanced curriculum gives you the tools to generate who you want to become. Even if imaginary, it is this purposeful three-day inquiry that leads you to focus your life for a meaningful outcome. At the conclusion of the course, I would declare before the group of participants the following statement: "From nothing, who I am is the possibility of power, love, and full self-expression; what I am giving up is that I cannot be loved." It was two months after this course when I would no longer be single. I had been in brief relationships, but this time, I would meet someone for good.

In a follow-on seminar series back in Brisbane, the seminar leader asked the participants what we each wanted for our lives. I eagerly raised my hand, stood up when requested, and said, "A relationship!" Within a week or two, I was at the Tuesday night venue for modern jive when I asked a girl with straight, long black hair for a dance. Her name was Jen. At first, my confidence was mistaken for arrogance and she truthfully told me how I came across to women. I asked Jen on a date, and although my energy and courage might have been attractive, my single way of splitting bills was a turn-off. I found it to be a real challenge to win her heart, and she raised my standards to keep up with hers, which were naturally learned and practiced. After six months, I did win her heart, and to put it simply, she is by far my better half.

While Landmark altered my destiny, Jen altered my universe. With her, I have gotten to play the role of the masculine protector and be everything in a couple that I had never experienced before. Things such as taking walks in the park, practicing *tai chi*, learning beginner's Mandarin, and traveling overseas every year for ten years to visit her extended family in the Philippines have brought us closer together. I have been adopted into her family unit with the love and support that Jen has inspired them to give me. What they often lack in finances, they are rich with love and family bond.

The simple things in life are the ultimate pleasures, such as food and togetherness as humans, things we are often impoverished of in western countries. In the Philippines, you can walk the local street outside your house and buy food made by your neigbours. You are not long on your own in this part of the world; people like to spend a lot of their time outside and amongst other people.

I have thankfully experienced many adventures, weddings, a funeral, and a lot of celebrations because of the closeness of my partner to her family. After 12 years and only ever being apart from each other for a week, our love and support have crystallized our relationship.

I have shared many happy days in my life with this young lady, but none grander than the birth of our son, Ethan, who is now three. We sometimes wonder how our life together was so good before and how much time we must have wasted, as having our own child, a creation from love, has added a new plane of existence—a new dimension—to our individual roles and has made us a part of the parenting community where we could finally relate to our friends who also have children. The blessings have been tenfold, and our former life seems a distant memory.

Life carries with it many moments of anxiety or fear about what is coming your way. For instance, when our second child was in the womb, I could not imagine how much love Jen and I would have for our little princess before she was born. But we have pure love for our new baby girl, and we would never have known of this feeling had we not taken a chance in love.

I truly believe that personal development, whether voraciously reading books, listening to YouTube or audiobooks, or attending seminars with like-minded people on topics like neuro-linguistics programming, yoga, meditation, and transformation can help those who are stuck because of what is happening in their minds. There is a time to understand the past, but let it not be your default if it does not serve you. Seek to create your future whether with baby steps on your own or with the guidance of a coach.

Be inspired by the thought that love can have any meaning you want it to have—acceptance, to be happy with something, or beyond. Self-love is the greatest currency to living a fulfilled life as you generate love for yourself and others; what you inspire towards yourself you bring out in those around you.

"The essence of spirituality is universal love."

~ Anthony Williams

CHAPTER NINE

❖

Alignment

By Annie Pearson

For me "Returning to Love" has been about returning to alignment with my true, authentic self and love of myself. It is about returning to our core, our whole and complete self before we go on into life and get shattered, unaligned, fractured, and, for some, broken into pieces. All the while trying to fit into and navigate this world as we try to please people and to be what everyone and everything seems to be telling us to be, telling us we should be or need to be or shouldn't be.

Returning to Love and/or the part of alignment where we love ourselves, for me, feels solid, grounded, secure, stable, whole, and complete. It makes making choices and decisions so much easier.

Returning to love for and of myself gave me the strength and unwavering conviction to make a decision that would bring another level of magical love to my life—the decision to go ahead and have a child on my own by a donor.

At 41, despite being $47,000 in debt, with no real secure business or job, living week-to-week in a share house, no savings, just debt, I didn't take too long to decide I was going ahead. I knew there would be challenges and all the what-ifs. And, oh, didn't everyone want to tell me the what-ifs! So often I heard, "What if this terrible thing happens or that terrible thing happens?"

I had, however, an unwavering knowing that I could do this. I knew I could bring a child into this world because I felt rock solid in who I was as a person and who I was becoming. I felt aligned and on track. I knew I still had a lot of learning, healing, and growing to do but I loved myself and I knew I was enough. I say solid and aligned enough because, as I've since discovered, there are many more beautiful levels and elements to *alignment* and love for self than I knew about then.

I felt aligned enough within myself mentally and emotionally to give that child my all. And by 'all' I mean a balanced all. I was blessed with an amazing mother who was so solid for us (my brothers, father, and I), and I wanted to be that for my child. (Sorry,

Dad, amazing father, too, of course!) I wanted to be in a position so that I could be solid for my child and myself no matter what lay ahead, a stable place from which to support and guide a child. I have witnessed all too much the impacts unbalanced parents have on children and know that parents who are not secure within themselves cannot truly put their children first, because they still need to fill their own gaps.

Rewind five years and there was no way I could or would have brought a child into this world on my own.

As I've mentioned, there are many levels and many approaches to alignment. On a simple level, there is aligning our diets, our bodies, our fitness. Our actions and behaviors with our values and dreams: congruency, as the great Tony Robbins says. And at a higher level, there is aligning our minds and beliefs with our subconscious. Our purpose, our hearts, our souls, and then some. My point is, there are so many levels to alignment. Diet and body alignment alone has each organ, each part of the body, let alone all the other parts of us.

I worked for years on so many elements. They all pulled me forward, toward alignment in some way. I started with small steps, making sure I exercised and slept well. I worked with a lot of mindset stuff, including exercises on my purpose and values, etc. The exercises were all valuable and did move me forward, but it seemed to be one step forward, two steps backward, and for the most part, I had to force myself do this stuff out of desperation. It wasn't, however, until I went to work directly on my self-worth that the solidness and love for myself kicked in. Instead of having to make myself do things, I *wanted* to do things. I was starting to value who I was, choosing what I did or didn't do. Things became a lot clearer.

From my experience and what I have learned since, I do believe that if you go straight for your core first, i.e., your self-worth and your self-love, and work directly on healing/reconnecting/realigning that first, then you have a true, solid center or place to work from for all the peripheral elements and levels of alignment. You feel centered, more empowered and worthy, even excited about working on other areas of alignment. It is my experience that, when our self-worth is aligned, many of the old self-sabotaging strategies we've developed to get by and survive life on fall away and become obsolete. Of course, there is still work to be done but when it is from a true, solid foundation you can begin to work progressively and forward. Like it's known to be with children, if they are provided a mentally, emotionally, and physically secure and safe place to develop, they can thrive and use their energy and focus on moving forward and not sideways, or nowhere, as they would when they have to use their energy searching for that security and safety.

I should clarify that self-worth has nothing to do with monetary worth or value.

Now, all that said, maybe I needed to go through the pain and struggle working on the peripherals to get to a place where I was open enough to work directly on my self-worth. I'm pretty sure this idea was presented and available to me all along in every book, every course, every teaching or lesson, but I couldn't see or hear it. I am also very familiar with the debilitating state of deep depression and anxiety, the kind where we can feel paralyzed and at times just barely capable of getting out of bed or doing anything, for that matter. For me, I was in a state where I needed to just do something—anything—that might pull me forward even a little.

The other thing to add here, very well explained by Dr. Michael Bernard Beckwith, is the concept of Kensho vs Satori. Kensho is growth by pain, and Satori is growth by awakening and/or insight. The majority of my shifts in the earlier days before working on my self-worth came from pain, struggle and desperation. I'd have a breaking point or reach a point where I'd had enough. After having worked on my self-worth, I started to get the hang of this deliberate and conscious creation. I began to do things the Satori way—hallelujah—doing little painless, even fun, boot camps and rituals for myself without having to wait for things to be at a breaking point or needing to struggle before doing something.

And so my story goes...at 35, I woke up—literally in sweat and terror—because I also woke up *consciously*. I was alert, very present, and very aware of where my life was in that moment. With an overwhelming feeling of *What the f#ck, What the f#ck have I been doing with my life, What the f#ck am I doing with my life, How the f#ck did I get to be 35 and...have nothing to my name.* I was in colossal debt (again), living week by week in struggle, smoking my head off and despising myself for it, regularly feeling hungover, and just, in general, going absolutely fucking nowhere. All of this, and I was already thirty-fucking-five.

I'd always said, if I hadn't met the man of my dreams by 35, I'd just go ahead and have a child on my own. Well, I was sure in no state to bring a child into this world—not financially and, more importantly, not emotionally or mentally.

I had come a long way. I'd spent my life between the ages of 23 and 29 in a grey cloud of self-doubt and fairly deep depression and anxiety. I'd lost every ounce of confidence I had in myself to a relationship that had slowly whittled away at my self-esteem until there was absolutely none left. This was compounded and perpetuated by the shame and guilt I felt from having been unfaithful in my previous relationship and for which I felt that maybe I deserved to feel like I did.

I am grateful now for this experience, despite the many grey and painful years. It made me eventually question who I was and who I wanted to be and to find the path back to realignment and love for myself. The truth is, I was probably a time bomb waiting to go off. While I was blessed to have a loving, caring family life, society and the generation I grew up in was about fitting in, conforming, being a good girl, not rocking the boat. It was about picking a "good career".

Certainly, not about following our hearts and be true to ourselves. Not in the way I know now.

At 29, I got a glimpse of light, a memory of happiness, while standing out in my backyard smoking my head off, because that's what I did then—not liking myself—being and feeling exhausted and so drained and sick of being in this grey cloud of depression and anxiety. I was second-guessing everything I did, feeling so confused. I was feeling alone. It was heavy and exhausting. Questioning myself in desperation and searching for what and how I wanted to feel. Happy came to mind and I said almost out loud, "I want to feel happy." It may seem crazy to many and of course does to me now, that Happy is not an obvious and or automatic choice. I am so thankful I had experienced what happy felt like as a child and teenager with my family, as many, I now know, never have and or they do not feel worthy of happiness. Not sure I felt worthy of it either at the time, but I knew that feeling, albeit very distantly at the time.

I started to explore, inquire, get curious about, and learn more about Happiness. I started to practice some of the things I'd learned. I heard Marci Shimoff, the author of *Happy for No Reason,* on the radio talking about things you can do to bring more happiness into your life. The idea that I felt I could take on at the time was going to bed before 10 p.m., ideally 9 p.m., three nights in a row. She said that an hour before midnight is worth two hours of sleep after midnight and said we should try it and see what happens. Through resistance and desperation, I tried it, I had to do something. It was quite profound. I had a clearer head and more energy, and I even felt happy about the day ahead.

Sounds so obvious to me now, but at the time I was lucky I got through the grey clouds in my head.

The memory of happiness helped my head and heart lift from the cloud; there was color around me. I met some beautiful kind-hearted girls and we became a close-knit group that continued to party together and have lots of good-hearted fun. My world was bright and full of laughs and good moments most of the time. I was feeling back to myself, alive again. I felt me beneath the clouds.

When things slowed down or stopped, the clouds were there. I was able to ignore or block out or avoid the clouds most of the time by staying busy with work or being out partying and getting drunk. Sundays, however, were my dark days. I called them my black Sundays, as I felt alone and annoyed at myself—a combination of being hungover and living under grey clouds. I learned to ride out my Sundays.

The pain, the loneliness, confusion, and annoyance at myself, combined with and perpetuated by being hungover, had my emotions and head churning all over the place. It was like my brain and all my feelings were being tossed around in a washing machine. I would just tell myself, "Hold on." It felt like holding on for dear life. If I could hold on and remind myself that this day would be over soon, that it was just one day and that it would be Monday soon and everything would be all right. I knew I would be able to get busy with work or go out for drinks throughout the week and those feelings would go away or, at least, I would be able to avoid them. The good times kept rolling, and they were fun.

I did learn to make myself get out and walk on Sundays. It helped if I woke up and was still drunk, so that the hangover hadn't quite kicked in, and with a bit of luck, I could walk the hangover or alcohol off before it got into my head. At least if I walked the hangover off, I was then just dealing with the grey clouds. A hangover would fuck with my mind so much more, but it took me a while to work that out—another *der* moment. I made a declaration that I would stop drinking and going out as much. It was like something inside me got terrified of letting go of my hiding space, and I got worse for the next few years before I got better. Any step forward back then seemed like it was always one step forward and two steps backward. I had so much doubt in myself.

I was happier within myself, or at least on the surface. It was, or seemed, just the money or lack thereof, such as debt and living week-to-week, that appeared to be weighing me down.

Another 2.5 years of that struggle and pain, and I was 37.5 years old. I had managed to pull back a little from going out, so I had the occasional weekend without a hangover, but my black Sundays were still there.

A good friend told me that I had a bad association with money and should have a look at it.

I went along to a free weekend seminar, T Harv Eker's Millionaire Mind Intensive, and walked out of it having purchased the Quantum Leap series of courses for $10K. This was $10K I did not have, nor did my credit cards, so I put it on a payment plan and prayed it would work. I did not dare to tell my family or anyone close to me who wasn't open to personal development. I knew most would think I was crazy, spending money I did not have, let alone on personal development. It has been absolutely the best $10K I have spent to date. I invested in myself and opened the door that led me back to what I really needed.

T Harv Eker's courses and brilliant team—Alex Mandossian, Blair Singer, Marjean Holden, all had the same underlying message: Really at the core of it all was our mindset and self-worth, and the need to align the two. If we have no money, that reflects our money blueprint but, more so, our self-worth.

It was about getting true to ourselves, tapping into and uncovering—or realigning ourselves with—who we were at heart and core. It was about learning to value ourselves and our unique gifts, to identify and get aligned with our purpose, our contribution, etc. It was about getting beneath the layers of what society and generations had conditioned us to accept and believe and unraveling who we are and who we want to be, what we want to do, and what we want to have.

The courses are designed to draw all of this out and give us the belief and tools to be daring enough to follow our dreams, knowing that others may not believe in us or support us and our ideas. It was all about alignment with our true selves and combining that with business strategies to leverage our unique gifts and gold and create lives we love for ourselves. We learned to distinguish between real and false fear, our own self-doubt and self-talk, both the supportive and unsupportive. It was about unlocking our creativity and enabling us to continue on, despite the tough and challenging times and ups and downs that life and business will bring.

> **"Daring to set boundaries is about having the courage to love ourselves, even when we risk disappointing others."**
> ~ Brené Brown

One of the courses was run by the marketing guru, Joel Roberts. On one of the days, he brought me up on stage and proceeded to rip through me because, when he'd asked us what we did, I'd put my hand up and shared. At the time, I thought I was cool and funny saying, "I'm a bookkeeper. It keeps me off the street and out of trouble." Well, he spent the rest of the day and half of the next morning ripping me to pieces. He did it in a fun, gentle, yet direct way as an example to everyone. It was exactly what I needed to hear. He said, "If that is the way you are talking about what you do, honey, you are not serious, and you are going to get nowhere fast."

I won an opportunity to attend Larry Gilman's Mastery of Self Expression, another fabulous course. At the end of the session, Gilman asked us to write down what we were committed to and said, "And don't write down what you say you are committed to but you are not really doing anything about." These gurus were so good at calling us out. Caught! Another ouch moment of being honest with myself. The truth was, I wasn't committed to anything seriously—another great reality slap in the face.

I returned home making a real decision. That was it; I stopped going out, quit smoking, and had to either get serious and committed to my business or get out there and get a job, and I didn't want a job. I wanted a life.

I called a friend and brainstormed about what I was doing or could do with my business. For the first time, I was feeling motivated and excited about my business, but money was still a struggle. I was nearly at rock bottom and wondering how I was going to pay my next week's rent. I'd just listened to the audio of Dr. Robert Anthony's *The Secret of Deliberate Creation* and, among many things, he'd explained the 17-

second Flip Switch. I'd learned the whole what-you-focus-on-is-what-you-get. I sure was focused on having no money: the "not enough" syndrome. I knew that's exactly what I was going to get more of unless I shifted my thinking. It's pretty damn hard not to focus on the reality that you actually have no money. I could feel the terror rising. The idea of the Flip Switch is to break your focus (vibration) on the struggle by switching your attention to something that makes you feel good and just for 17 seconds. Sounds easy, right? Well, it is and it isn't. This time I did it. I had to.

Every time I caught myself focusing on the terror of it all, I'd think of my new carpet. My flatmates and I had put a new piece of carpet in the lounge room. It had cost 50 bucks from a discount place and, oh, it made a difference! It was beautiful and it did make me feel happy when I saw or thought of it, so I would shift my focus to the carpet. Sound crazy or hilarious? Well, it worked amazingly. Not only did I start to feel better, luck came my way. I was offered a contract job within a few weeks, which saved my bacon and got me to a stable place.

It took me another Kensho moment to get to the next step. It was April 2012, and I was 39. My brother and sister-in-law had just had a baby, so we all flew to meet my new niece. I'd managed to scrape together enough funds to get up there somehow. At the time, I was still living week-to-week with credit cards maxed out. Looking back, I have no idea what I did with my money. I remember lying upstairs on my bed feeling broken, ashamed, lost, and terrified again at the reality of my financial and life situation. At least I was aware of it by this time instead of putting my head in the sand. My money situation just didn't seem to be getting any better, and I was starting on the downward spiral.

Come on; I had done enough of the work with T Harv Eker's Quantum Leap Program, well the theory of it. I was aware of the money mindset enough to realize that mine was one of scarcity, never having enough. I'd heard a lot that your money mindset is a reflection of your self-worth.

At the time, I had rejected that. I was seemingly confident. Well, I was socially confident, so I rejected the idea that I didn't feel worthy, and I felt insulted. I was lying there again, feeling terrified and sick of struggling, drained from stressing about never having enough money. I did not want to burden anyone or let anyone know, so I was hiding it— another exasperated 'enough' moment.

Something had to change. It seemed that everyone or everything had been telling me that it's all about self-worth. I didn't think it was, but what the f... I was going to take that on and do whatever was required to shift that bastard of a feeling and situation. I made up my mind that when I got back, I was going to actually do the things we'd learned—how to reprogram our minds, beliefs, neuropathways etc.—applying all of it to my beliefs about myself and money.

Upon my return to Melbourne, I immersed myself. I threw myself into it daily—actually two or three times a day for weeks. I did the affirmations in the morning. I YouTubed hypnotism and affirmations before I went to bed, and when I woke up, I did affirmations with the physical kinesthetic exercises we'd been taught. I was reprogramming not only my mind but my body memory, too. I did tapping, Margaret Lynch's method for attracting $50,000, which I will say was not just about the money, but was more about the beliefs we had about ourselves around money and life. I listened to the John Kehoe's *Mind Power* DVDs and learned more about how our trickster minds work to sabotage us. I did *ho'oponopono*, forgiving myself. I wrote 'I am enough' with lipstick on my bathroom mirror. I immersed myself. I didn't fully understand it at the time, but I just committed, trusted, or hoped like hell it would work.

Funny, I initially felt false to be hypnotizing myself, and I then reminded myself that I actually hadn't chosen who I was or the beliefs I had around money or myself or all kinds of things and so I took control and started to rewire my brain. My program that had been running me and my life was one created by others, society, old family values and cycles, or reactions passed on, perceptions or misperceptions we make as children that form our belief systems. While I was lucky to have parents who were open to us being who we wanted to be--to a degree—it was still a time when society imposed its own expectations of what I now know to be very limiting beliefs. So, here I was getting to choose my program and who I wanted to be, and the penny dropped.

Now, if only it could be that easy. Again, I'd learned this stuff and knew what to do. My subconscious and results did start to change. I realized one day that I wasn't stressing about money anymore. I had managed to get my finances in order. Oh, I still had debt, $47,000 of it, but weirdly it wasn't bothering me. I had a plan and was paying it off and felt confident that I was on the right track. My mind had shifted, and

I was pumped and excited and hungry for more learning, more growth. More self-respect. More Love.

Finally, a Satori Moment

I was reading Way of the Peaceful Warrior by Dan Millman, and I was heading up to Queensland to be with my parents over Christmas. Inspired by the book and knowing how the immersion and commitment had worked for me, I decided I was going to do a little boot camp for myself while I was in Queensland with my parents. I informed them that I would meditate for one hour every day while I was up there for the 12 or so days. They were, as usual, a little leery, as if to ask, "What's she up to now?" In their usual nonchalant way, they were open yet a little wary not wanting to be too encouraging in case it was some crazy cult thing.

I had read Eckhart Tolle's fantastic book *The Power of Now* and, as usual, totally got it in theory. I had practiced it a little, or dabbled, including doing a short meditation here and there and learning about the various approaches. My understanding was that it wasn't necessary to stop thinking; it was more about observing the thoughts. I just had to notice my thoughts, i.e., catch myself thinking or drifting off into thought, observe the thought, and then bring myself back to the mark I had picked out to focus on. I surprised myself and did it. It was only 12 or 15 days and, although I have done other various meditations along the way, this really sealed it in for me.

Learning and embedding the practice of being able to observe my thoughts and the practice of getting into the immediate present helped me observe and become aware of the unsupportive thoughts along with the ability to interrupt my thinking and redirect it to more supportive thoughts that were in line with my core. I've found it to be so true, as Eckhart Tolle explains, that there are no problems in the Now, just situations. There is no good or bad, no judgment in the now. Everything just is—no past or future to compare it to or be worried or fearful about.

In February of 2014, I discovered the #100HappyDays Challenge. While reading about the challenge, I learned that, while most people say they want to be happy, they aren't prepared to do something as simple as taking a picture every day, for 100 days, of something that makes them feel happy.

At this stage, I was pretty happy with who I was and where I was at most of the time. Although I was still having mini terror moments about my financial situation and other worries and was still waking a little dark some mornings or feeling a bit lost on weekends, I was feeling relatively stable in who I was and where I was going, all the same. I was always banging on to everyone about happiness, so I thought I'd better do this one and it sounded fun.

Easy to start with, I took pictures of sunsets and sunrises when I was getting up to go for my morning walk—images of blue skies and green grass. Towards the middle and end, I began to find the little day-to-day things that made me happy, things like my showerhead—or rather the hot water that came out of it. My shower head was pretty good, too. It was one of those awesome ones that cover you nicely and at an excellent pressure. And I loved my glasses that enabled me to see things clearly from a distance, glad wrap that allowed me to keep some of my favorite foods fresh and edible until the next day. Oh, and clean sheets, my red pants I bought for a bargain at the op shop, my blue pants I'd bought for a bargain at the op shop. My thongs (for the non-Aussies, my flip-flops, not my G-strings), walking and, of course, my amazing family and friends.

It wasn't until a while afterwards that I realized I was feeling awesome when I woke, fresh and energized and generally optimistic, basically feeling great and no longer were my weekends black. While I haven't had any medical or scientific testing to prove it, I do believe—and the science does seem to back it up—practicing gratitude daily does rewire the neuropathways of the brain. Which essentially is what I was doing each day.

I'm pretty sure this helped put me physically, mentally, and emotionally into a functional space that helped me with the next step of my journey, including falling pregnant the first time.

It was around June of that year when I got a call from a girlfriend. After we had a chat and giggle, she said "So, I was telling (let's say John) that I knew you wanted to have kids and he said he'd help you out." She quickly said, "Not sex, but that he said he would donate his sperm." We went on to giggle and laugh about having a sperm party. Still, at the end of the conversation, she said, "But, seriously, will you think about it? You are 41."

The seed was planted. I had been feeling great with where I was at, who I was being and where I was going. I had been also going through the thought process dealing with the fact that maybe I wasn't meant to have children in this lifetime. I had been secretly praying for some kind of miracle but knowing—thinking I was a long way from meeting a man, being in a relationship, and deciding to have a baby together. I would want to know someone quite well before entering into a serious relationship with him, let alone having a child together. I knew this was better to do either not at all or on your own if you're not in a supportive relationship. I think I'd forgotten about my declaration all those years ago: "If I haven't met the man of my dreams by the time I'm 35, I'm just going to go ahead and have a child on my own."

Long story short, I thought about it for a week or so, talked with a girlfriend, and decided to ask a guy I had dated who was a nice guy but not relationship material. He'd had his heart broken, among other things, and was not open to a relationship, not the kind I wanted anyway. I'd met his sisters, brother-in-law, and in particular his nieces and nephews who, to me, had a real nice groundedness about them which made me feel he had a good family. So, I asked if he would consider being a donor and left him to think about it. I checked in a week or so later, and he said he'd do it.

My parents weren't exactly over the moon with my plans. Mom, who is usually at least open to things, was not what I'd call excited. My dad said in a firm voice, "It's maybe not such a good idea." To which I said, "Well, you can either support me if you like or not, but, if not, I just won't talk to you about it." I was doing it whether they liked it or not.

I was so lucky and fell pregnant the first go, and I attribute it to maybe luck but mostly to the work I did earlier that put me in an awesomely aligned space, both mentally and emotionally, for it to happen. And, in April 2015, when I was 42 years old, my beautiful, healthy little awesome bundle of joy was born with, I might add, my mom and dad in the labor ward with me. Thankfully, they'd come down to be with me for the birth and to help me through the first six weeks. My beautiful boy is now five years old and an absolute joy.

Man, have I learned some stuff along the way and know I still have so much more to learn! I am excited to continue with learning and growing every day. Talk to me about the parenting learning journey – that is another story—one full of challenges but a beautiful one.

What's next?

I am very passionate about creating an even more awesome life for myself and my son and the world. I am working on my human potential and passionate about supporting others to become aware of and to allow their own.

I am excited for myself, my son, and the world, because things that have been taboo in the mainstream are now starting to be talked about, accepted or acknowledged, and more widely understood, such as all of the mental health stuff, trauma, gender inequality, shame, and the impact these things have on all of our lives when society keeps them as taboo. So many, if not all of us, have our self-worth shattered in the early years of our lives, and the causes are not yet accepted or understood in the mainstream.

I'm excited, because whilst this kind of stuff is being taught to adults and the wider communities, it is also being taught to our children, giving them a fighting chance to develop the self-love and self-worth and tools to help them avoid and or overcome such obstacles and to stay aligned with a solid, centered self-worth no matter what.

While my journey has seemed debilitating and excruciating at times, I know it is nothing compared to what so many have suffered and experienced in the way of trauma. At the same time, I think it's important not to diminish or disregard the seemingly minor challenges we may have gone through, or might now be going through, by comparing our own situations to those of others. These things are still painful and it can be a struggle to get our heads and spirits around so that we can work out our difficulties and how we can align ourselves with the love for ourselves—love that is within and always there.

I do want to shout to the world, and I do plan to. Let's get everyone to heal and align with their true self-worth! I genuinely believe there will be less crime, less unnecessary hurt, less pain, less anger in the world. There would be less drug and alcohol addiction—or any addiction for that matter. I do think a lot of people might leave their jobs, relationships, and other situations with a new knowing that they are worthy of love and being treated better, worthy of being heard and respected. I do believe that life for more people would be a lot happier, more fun, with a lot more open collaboration and creativity, and mostly a lot more love for ourselves and others.

The information, education, and awareness that is coming to light and is being shared and talked about has challenged and is breaking the old molds of the old bullshit institutions, religious, and cultural beliefs. This is awesome. There are so many, as Vishen Lakhiani, founder of Mindvalley and author of *The Code of the Extraordinary Mind*, calls them 'BRULES'—bullshit rules—being exposed and broken, including those that shamed women for having children out of wedlock, let alone on their own.

What I am most excited about is that it is possible for everyone and anyone—even for those with the deepest wounds—to heal, align, return to love, and to thrive!

"Worthy now. Not if. Not when. We are worthy of love and belonging now. Right this minute. As is."
~ Brené Brown

"To forgive is the highest, most beautiful form of love. In return you will receive untold peace and happiness."

~ Robert Muller

CHAPTER TEN

❖

Aham Brahmāsmi

अहम् ब्रह्मास्मि

"I am the Absolute"

By Mia Paul

I t is one of the four Mahavakyas, these are "The Great Sayings" of the Upanishads, as characterized by the Advaita school of Vedanta, used to explain the unity of the macrocosm and the microcosm.

I stand silently in my hushed life near the old port of Marseille.

I feel the weight of the wooded hillside fortified behind me.

I climb slowly out of my calf skin jacket and light a cigarette; it hangs lazily from my sleeping lips.

Fragrant oils ignite beneath a coral moon and anoint me.

The arrival of fishermen scents the wharf with sardines and sea bass.

I think of sheltering ports laden with treasures; of small boats corroded by shrewd men carrying hearts filled with muddy despair, singing songs of sorrow and weariness from nostalgias they could not escape.

I lick my salt encrusted lips gripping the fuss of an Octopus stew made of plum wine from the hot springs. Gauchely dressed in clams and cilantro, sweet fruits and aperitif wines that once reached the table of Tsars. A lingering banquet masked by tenderness.

My arms bandage my torso gracelessly as a humid plainness seeps through my thawing body. The night covers the rough unsophisticated remains of loss and conflict, of the port's crude stench, centuries accumulated.

The night whispers a resonating litany of mythical oaths.

I have come to where the moons and lovers play to escape the reach of slavish pride.

A full moon illuminates the deepening skies bringing life and serenity to my shadows.

I exhale and reflect as I bow my head and sway.

A soft whisper echoes, 'shhhhhhhhhhhhhh…don't wake me'

I fall fearlessly into the depths of my imagination where magic and memory mix.

Etched deep by nature's hand, I feel the scar on my face polished by the winds incessant touch.

A fragment of mirrored glass tears my shoeless foot.

I am awakened to a sense of menace. No longer asleep in my calm black stream.

I feel open eyes on my skin…

The night dense with impenetrable fog. A form appears.

A car, dark, stolen, bruised. A door swings open, I am sucked in.

The sound of men and engines pierce my quiet ears.

A boy presses his face hard against my lips; his noxious touch scrapes my skin like a spatula grazed from years of guilt and tattooing.

From his filthy, unwell body shine the bluest eyes, swollen from unknown grief.

A faded smile grips his cheek, his gaze haunting.

He grabs me with bulky, waterless hands squeezing my shrunken face and with a rumbling growl exhales his heat into my mouth and swallows me.

His claws dig deep into my flesh, my heart stolen on the waterfront tearing it from the dusty soil where it once stood, naked for the world to see.

A gust of wind strips me of my loosening sanity, I pray it will wipe my conscience clean.

I cannot destroy or civilize him.

Pressed hard against him, I am divided forever.

I speak, my words like a blade taken hastily to the heart. I push clumsily with a rush of hate, a ripple bleeds bloodlessly from him; it makes him neither lover nor ally nor admirer.

His breath drowns me, a swarming rage, leaving no room for influence or sovereignty.

I start to quiver; palpitations cramming my chest, tears flood my sodden face, sobbing, snivelling I start to moan intrusively.

His face turns to stone, crushed I begin to weep.

I cry and cry unbreakably whimpering like a percussive instrument, capacious, a musical diaspora.

I am dragged to a flawless façade of French architecture.

On the other side seven stories of stone and rubble, wreckage and betrayal.

The night frost bites deep into my skin, dividing darkness from dawn.

I am raped by five; they make a sacrifice of my fat and bones.

Shackled to this rock face. Like Prometheus I am bound.

I know my torn flesh will not mend.

I raise my hands to my face guarding it from falling ashes, the sounds of spring fall mutely on my threadbare neck.

The access to my mythical world now closed.

Low in a lip pursed whisper, I think out loud.

'Death comes as a maniac, mine while I am awake.'

I lay, emaciated as blood spills delicately from my blackened body.

I am 18

When you look inside me, this is what you will find.

The Book of Secrets ~

On my first solo trip to Europe I was raped.

The first of three violent rapes that took five decades to expel.

Living in Berlin, I did not share this with anyone except my boyfriend and his mother, a nurse who saved me from collapse.

I now wholly comprehend the subtle and lingering force of harbouring this incursion.

My entire vagina was torn and ruptured and needed to be reconstructed. For a time, I lost all flexibility and sensation. As our society is so enamoured with vulgar terms of expression concerning the vagina, I rarely spoke about it, infusing my healing with more hinderance. Today I know the 'Yoni' to be a symbol of sexual gratification and a matrix of creation.

It remained difficult for me to have any sexual encounters without irritation, so I chose a life of virtual aloneness that I am still intending to alter.

I was a beautiful young woman, with a creative, spiritual and physical vision for my future.

I was already experiencing a connection to the celestial realm that was indefinable, but my once spiritual sensitivities were being swamped by rage that had previously lain dormant. I received a lot of discrimination at school as a dark skinned, first generation Greek-Cypriot. This started a lifelong story of persecution and victim consciousness.

It did not take long for my child-teen innocence to be consumed and distorted by a defiant anarchist. I became a new breed of warrior looking to tattoo the loudest scream of my irreplaceable presence for all to see. Lost in a dense heap of oppressed energies and experiences, a disturbing, weeping avalanche was set in motion.

I lost all emotional presence. Withdrawing into aloneness, a rendered indifference made me aloof and strangely captivating. As 'validation' was and is a crucial social currency, my arrogance was a magnet for others to resolve their own self-doubt. My seduction lured others into a seeping truth that smothered us all, until all the truths became one undistinguishable lie.

Irrespective, I was still terrified to engage in any authentic intimacy.

Agitated and unable to find true vocal expression I altered myself and became entirely androgynous. Layered in black, I was able to conceal my true physical and emotional emaciation.

I mistook secrecy for mystery. I resolved the fractal of my elevating grief with drugs and alcohol that were perilous and lethal.

Noisily bleeding from the soul, I became an egomaniac with low self-esteem, ruled by quieted fear and incessant sorrow. Easily deluded and governed by 'small mind' programming, I became reckless, unreliable, desperate, grandiose and pride driven. An undomesticated and entirely irreverent child. Sitting in adult bars dominated by moral elasticity, refusing to repent for her iniquities. A frail shell absorbing everything in its path to self-destruction.

There was a giant unfillable void in my body where my life used to be. I was no longer a whole person, only a shadowy memory. Most things were beyond the capacity of my human understanding. Everything and every day became immutable and I was entirely reticent to the angelic intelligence I once understood.

Those 'waterless hands' crushed my voice, repressing my authenticity until its subtle replay muted all my senses. Immune to both blame and praise, I kept blowing my own sorrowful trumpet for many years.

Ultimately, I inflicted such violence unto myself, I was untouchable and impossible to Love. Tearing accumulating memories of untamed cruelty from my heart and thrusting them clumsily overboard.

My childhood dream to be an artist and renowned, sabotaged. Art School, Punk and Berlin in the early 80's became my home, a majestic convergence of unadulterated chaos. I rejected the judgments and labels of others but relished my own branding and was a proud Art School Anarchist who 'sang' in forgotten punk bands filled with adolescents sharing drug ideologies.

This escalating disconnection would follow me into my mid-50s.

I had ripped open a wound that could not be satiated by anyone or anything. My consumption of people, places and things became desperate and chaotic. Unleashing wickedness and corruption that pierced my accomplices and pushed them down into a drowning sea. Every impulse conditional. I arrived like Pandora a fruitless blend of cunning, gold and dross, snow and mud, love and cruelty.

I created a 'throne' I was unfit to rule; I wanted to run away and sin in peace. Madness was engulfing me, disguised as secular and contagious lament. I was looking for solitude where I could harvest my unreasonable and groundless hope. In an attempt to be seen and successful, the virtues of my divine feminine, creation, intuition, community and sensuality were smothered by my 'inauthentic' masculine.

Once a fixture of stone, I started to crumble, reduced to a pile of salt. I picked up a broom and swept the last of its remains from my garden, as I exhaled into the wind I felt the loosening of its grip. I peered into the abyss of my own ambitions and found the city was not sculpted of pure gold.

This playground of hedonists I entranced was filled with lunacy. A life of chaotic measure, its unfolding almost fatal.

In 1987 in her 46th year my Divine mother, distinguished by exceptional courage and celestial grace, passed. We struggled in our lives to embrace one another as I imbued our story with self-created abandonment. She, however, never took her eyes off me, awaiting an opportunity to liberate me from this dehumanizing curve.

In my 28th year, on the cusp of my first Saturn Return, a gruesome rebirth arrived on a cold bathroom floor. I shook to my feet, my frozen lips and flesh embalmed blue. Aroused from death, by my deceased mother who pushed breath into my lungs. Saturn brought with it the burden of time, and the first recognition of my own mortality, forcing me to examine my true self and what I had manifested.

I was ready to move forward, but I had led the life of an infamous 'rock star'. Inciting exhausting demands, taking little personal responsibility and looking for endless absolution.

I sought to divorce myself from being trafficked as a woman, but I was still tainted by my own self-loathing and surrounded by a society of unguided anarchists, offering little guidance. I reached out to women who called themselves 'sisters' but received little support. This regurgitated my story of persecution that echoed my experience at school. I was a victim, not authenticated by violence, but self-made. Entombed by stories that intelligent, creative, beautiful and powerful women were not socially acceptable nor 'allowed' to succeed.

I just could not crack the shell of self-love. I didn't even know what it meant to love myself. I was immersed in a self-made mire that did not allow any infiltration. I knew nothing of love, only of force and violence that split the fibres of my being and tore me apart.

As engulfing and seemingly endless were those darker days, I slowly softened and incepted change. I accepted in secrecy I was a generous woman, with a ferocity of heart, who selectively embraced and protected her peers. I longed for a conscious contact with God and holistic abundance. If every tangible, sensory experience is an opportunity to incorporate loving intelligence, and the human experience is a vehicle for God to witness Itself, then who am I to judge or be judged? To judge is to enhance separation and float ceaselessly in forgetting.

I made an inner connection upon awakening, a newly forged understanding of free will that set-in motion a succession of choices to challenge my secrets and spiritual malaise.

Until I was ready to remember why I was here, in this life, and what my offering was, this disturbing rollercoaster was my path. It was not until years passed that I understood I had already written my story. Every time I felt any semblance of freedom or simplicity, I accepted I was meticulously remembering.

Exhausted by the addiction of alienation and transformation brought about by deterioration, I was ready to embrace change enthusiastically.

The Book of Awakening + Resistance ~

I was harassed by people into slowing down and taking form in the NOW. My resistance was excruciating. I was releasing a massive inventory of stress. It petrified me to let go of the narratives. I lived sporadic, fractured chapters, excelling swiftly, was rewarded, and departed before my elaborations were revealed. I had been running all my life and felt every grating edge brought about by the polarity of God and my human existence. Once I understood we are mystical, sacred, heavenly beings in a human experience I was punctured with fear. If all I am is a physical body on this planet's solid surface and that body is going to die, what would I contribute and accomplish before that point in time?

I had studied Fine Art, Fashion and Interior Design with the intention of prospering in those playgrounds. I hijacked my destiny and found I was not without creative skill, but entirely without purpose. I went through a temporary self-analysis about my chosen creative disciplines. Where they meaningless and indulgent? Today I revel in my creative offerings and see much of my ancestral lineage in their form.

It took time, but I rectified the distinction between my physical contributions and my eventual spiritual calling and found no sacred disparity.

I started to sense the spectrum of time simultaneously. I began to exist in and experience multiple dimensions at once, but if Love is a convergence of three timelines past, present and future, how would I attain that and what was the point of planning and purpose?

For the first time in my life I was a witness. I chose a path of sobriety, steadfast at the shore of an entirely transformed truth.

This critical choice to accept sobriety in all areas of my life became the foundation for the quest to come.

It gifted me the consciousness to understand the importance of service, self-responsibility, surrender and the significance of making amends. Fifteen years of sobriety unfolded to equal fifteen years of sabotage. I still live a life of virtual abstinence today, but I do not intimidate myself with harsh constraints.

This is the timeline where all of Love's anchors embalmed themselves into my being. I was guided by clarity born of my intuitive heart, a changed lucidity that catalysed at the precipice of this time of self-revelation. With great confidence and indomitable fortitude, I sought to help and liberate the lost and innocent. With a new patience and integration with the earth and all living things I started the long journey to self-Love, self-forgiveness and forgiveness and Love of others.

Essentially looking for redemption, I drank in all I could in an effort to erase who and what I had become. Eager for a complete metamorphosis I started with health and vitality for the body and mind. I adopted the mindsets of humility, compassion, tolerance, gratitude, philanthropy, service to others, and spiritual fitness as guided by yogic and qigong traditions. I immersed myself in Eastern philosophies, three Vipassana's a year for ten years. I spoke at self-help conventions to support individuals with addiction problems, offered personal sponsorship, gifted my time in women's prisons and rehabilitation institutions, volunteered to support the homeless, unemployed and socially isolated youth through wilderness escape camps, but I was still only the messenger.

Owing to my choices I had been and was still in conflict with my biological family and a long way from harmonious empathy and my true soul's nature.

I wanted to be instantly triumphant, and my awakening reinforced by immediate sensory bliss. Instead, I ricochet between angelic experiences and the woes of isolated depression, which were accumulating and re-occurring. It felt like a charade. Blindingly obvious was the illusory notion that we can manage deception, an idiom of the ego where all laws are broken.

It was a slow telling to witness beneath my good intentions was an ego that wished to be celebrated and gifted the greatest currency of our time, affirmation. Once the veils of distraction had been lifted social affirmation became my new drug. Sensitivity replaced indifference, servility, superiority, and the deepest anchor; people pleasing abolished rejection. I was a first-generation of immigrant parents who knew no social, ethical, inherited, or honourable integration, I felt entirely regressed striving for reassurance and survival in this way. Revisiting my first childhood struggles I was overrun with ignorance and a new insurgence of abandonment. This was a new kind of duplicity.

I sought to free myself from this new bondage of pre-occupation, attempting to no longer live as a victim and free myself from associated entrapments and limitations. This was the next step of my humanity and its imprint spawned a torrent of anger, resentment and conflict. I wasted countless hours imagining what other people thought of me, as my self-absorption intensified everything felt rehearsed and predictable, and my insecurity inevitably counteracted the briefest moments of pleasure. I endeavoured to implement effective boundaries and needed to learn how to do this without controversy.

I wanted to be transparent, and honour my principles and ideals, except I wasn't entirely sure what they were. Despite the natural order and joy that accompanied all positive action, I was still resistant and my efficiency at self-sabotage meant that joy came in increments; cocoons I would spin for protection in this pupal stage. I naturally wanted to be shielded and comforted after all that corrosion. I was a woman determined to unearth her wisdom but still experiencing repression and attitudes of discrimination. Love's anchors were still only sporadically within my reach and my intimate experience of Universal Love yet to be revealed.

I participated in uncountable spiritual offerings and was infinitely confused why I was still in struggle. I saw the recurrent cost of my behaviour and the trappings of those endless problems. The omnipresence of the spiritual realm that I now understand, still felt unattainable. I would witness God infrequently and yet to recall I had made a journey here from the stars. I was grasping at illumination but still felt the polarity and imbalance so deeply of living in separation. Still discontent with today, engrossed in yesterday and petrified of tomorrow.

Resolved to erase my shadows, I would continuously chisel away at myself. Idealistic expectations engraved deep into my skin. I recognized this was a disease that lead to more unhappiness and mortal delusion. I realised it was not about trying to get rid of or push away, it was about encompassing, leaning in, and making changes at the soul level. This was not something I could understand from the mind, it had to come from the heart centre. It was time to take full responsibility and embrace what has become one of my primary spiritual principles, reciprocity.

I was experiencing enough remembrance to know I could not continue my trajectory of entitlement, dodging metaphorical bullets, I just kept 'showing up' despite my resistance.

I had an opportunity to look at the wasteland of my adult life and love it with unconditional forgiveness. I became entirely honest; I took responsibility for the impact I had made and grounded it deep into the earth. I made amends proving my trustworthiness and squashed dissonance where light could not flow.

Through the wisdom of Vedic meditation, I became dedicated to seeing God in everything in my waking state, not through religion, but by revelation. This new faith led me to understand that Love already and always existed in me in the NOW.

I maintained a relentless commitment to transformation. I knew innately, what would be revealed was a miraculous phenomenon I could never have imagined. I immersed myself in meditation, which would ultimately liquify every uncertainty.

The Book of Clarity ~

I started to assimilate through teachings that change occurs WITHIN and the emancipation I sought from my past was not a tangible physical expression. I believed as humans, we would not be remembered for our words spoken despite their consuming and impactful capacity, but by the energy we emitted, because we are energy first. My energy imprint and boundary were increasing exponentially and my relationship to Gaia was grounded in this energetic reciprocation.

I became hungrier for things that our physical reality could not offer, an initiate desperately seeking illumination and spiritual nourishment. It took countless, painful teachings to genuinely admit this human experience is simply an illusion. A profoundly textural, tangible sensory experience of incredible virtuosity, but nevertheless an illusion. I was breaking the habit of being myself, channelling and remembering my soul's true dignity.

It took time to celebrate, a myriad of cycles continued to unfold before I truly inhabited the beauty of life. I sought enlightenment with such passion, but occasionally, still felt like a charlatan incapable of putting in any lasting action.

I sincerely wanted whatever needed to be broken within me to break, so I could entirely welcome this transformation. I needed to pry my heart open and feel humility and Love as more than just a mantra. My daily practice became nonnegotiable as I tested many spiritual offerings. I often forgot to breathe deeply and began breathwork which became a force that unified me and cracked the storm I was conducting wide open.

I returned to singing. Every time I sang a flush of the heart ornamented my entire being with impassioned vitality. The days of playing toy piano and screaming political threats in squalid squats were certainly over. Instead I joined Kirtan circles which practiced devotional singing in Hinduism, Vaishnava, Sikhism, the Sant traditions and some forms of Buddhism. I was able to amplify certain harmonics like those of the Tibetan monks, whose tantric chanting was polyphonic and invoked the deities they were praying to. I continue to participate in Kirtan, and it brings me pure, unadulterated joy. This remembrance aligned with my studies of the Vedas,

Puranas, Mahabharat, Ramayana and Upanishads
Hinduism.

The resonance of Hinduism was entirely profound for
me. This eternal tradition conceives of God as pure
Consciousness; omnipresent, omniscient and
omnipotent, in us always, in every other human being
and in the whole of creation. The goal is absolute
liberation from sufferance, attained through the
ethical foundation of Dharma, a set of associated
guidelines for behaviour. My spiritual practice to
transform the mind and be aware of God's presence
was my foundation for everything.

In my 56th year, at the end of my second Saturn Return
it was time to harvest what I had spiritually reaped.
Time to discard all which no longer served me and
prune its fragments. It was not another rebirth, but a
birthing of the higher self. It was time to consistently
raise the flag for truth and responsibility and stop
testing its elastic resistance. Time to heal the
distortions I had previously understood of gender and
discard the illusions of the inauthentic Divine
Feminine and Masculine.

An inspirational time to stand on solid ground, without
any more pretexts and disillusion.

I started to work with healers, psychic conduits and seers who channelled energy to help me connect with my ancestral families. I grasped the periodic visions that recurred in my youth were memories of other timelines, of other lives lived. My most persistent visions were as a golden eagle huntress, a female warrior of the windblown plains of the Gobi Desert. A Kazakh nomad living in the wilderness of the Altai region of far western Mongolia, characterized by its glacial lakes and snow-covered peaks. Hunters often sing to their eagles to get them used to their voice, during a session I recalled this exchange with my eagle that still reverberates in my expression today.

I was a tall, dark, lithe seductive creature characterised by my masculine grace. Entirely unique, I was disposed to reverie and imaginings. I rode over high mountain ridges, over rough and frozen terrains finding peace and inspiration in the vastness of my unhurried sanctuary.

I integrated many timelines in these sessions. Recurrent remembrances of sitting in council as 'Mother' in Atlantis which still remains a zenith role in my life today. According to Robert Sarmast, the submerged land mass of colossal buildings, bridges, canals, temples and artefacts to be found in the waters located off Cyprus's immemorial coast matches Plato's famed description of Atlantis almost perfectly.

I saw myself as an emissary of light, from the Pleiadian star system, guiding others beyond past limitations to take full spiritual responsibility and align with their soul connections.

At exactly this time three of my ancestral families went to war inside me, agitating my heartbeat until I was forced to wear a monitor to subdue speculation that I was destined for a heart attack. I would speak to a Vedic Astrologer who confirmed this Book of Saturn had ended and the 28-year cycle of disparate trauma was experienced and complete.

The most pinnacle clarity that correlates with the timeline of 2020, my 58th year, was disentangling myself from precarious ancestral contracts. Contracts I had written, and archaic choices I had made. This was the true indestructible face that led to the paradise of ascension. To be graced with neutrality, non-attachment and meditation for God-realization, entirely humbled and enriched me. I was finished with confusing nature and crafting separation from Source.

This was a liberation that forged a clear sense of purpose and my highest potential to be birthed. Finally, a flood of peace washed over me, I no longer judged myself for my foreboding anger and insensitivity in times of adversity. No longer ruled by my emotions and no longer reliant on cushions of light to feel joyful and at ease. Love arrived via people, places and things, the elixir and magical potion that would prolong my life.

It was a long journey to be able to hold the frequency of Universal Love in my daily life. A personal and Universal Love that comes with a sensory and timeless sweetness that bathes the body and mind in vitality and a passion for embracing every living thing. A return to Oneness and the purity of source. I felt the only truth was the presence of God and I understood that God was Love and Love was God and I am that too.

The Book of Fate ~

In 1962 the first slow activations of two of the planetary chakras, Mount Shasta - the Root Chakra and the great Pyramid and the Sphinx - the Throat Chakra, attracted new types of souls to planet Earth, souls with a higher spiritual divine blueprint and purpose. These two earth centres of consciousness drew forth these forerunners and pioneers of the Age of Aquarius.

They arrived with a revolutionary purpose, as part of the first wave of builders and creators transcending the passage from the era of Pisces to Aquarius. Incarnated with a strong determination to shift old paradigms and bring an end to the slavery of 'self-service' and 'control over'. As Emissaries of Light, they came to share their life and creative process with others as teachers and guides. To bond the cornerstones of the Age of Aquarius, preparing the path for the next wave of souls coming to earth in this Millennium.

I am born February 14th, 1962 of Greek Cypriot descent and always felt this imprint in my being.

I adopted many teachers, but not until I studied the Vedas as inferred by Maharishi Mahesh Yogi who brought Transcendental meditation to the West, did I understand the faint remains of ignorance were revisited in the process of deleting them. I decided to stop embracing ignorance and enact a final chapter of self-forgiveness or this cycle of disorientation would never cease. I sought reverence for the level of consciousness I and each person embodied and released all condemnation. Who was I to judge another's story? It became evident my inclination to judge myself and others was an act of avoidance to prevent myself from self-forgiveness and accepting the choices I made brought longevous hardship. Forgiving myself for being the victim of the rape/s and for all the accumulated conflicts that previously lingered like unwashable stains on my life. My belief in rebirth alleviated the fear of a final conviction based on this life alone. I am reminded by Karmic law the causal link between action and consequence.

By my early 50's I was ready to retreat to the forest to meditate and stop all verbal communication. I had taken vows of silence before and am currently committed to an unlimited timeframe as I write this chapter, silence, where the mind and senses are silent, but Cosmic Consciousness is fully awake. Meditation continues to be my elixir; it has opened me up to teachings and mantras that tickle the subtle centres of my superconscious and shower me in a thousand rays of cascading light.

Brahman, in the Hindu tradition is the Totality, the ubiquitous, unbounded, eternal truth and bliss, unchanging, yet the cause of all change. I was/am ready to transcend the 'dream' that was my life and embrace God Consciousness and cognize a lasting truth.

I began to transcend the relative, to establish myself in 'being' and take action. At any given point in each shift of consciousness where the Knower, Knowing and the Known merge, I would experience all realties at once, where omnipresence yields omniscience.

Change started to assimilate and enrich all areas of my life.

In the latter half of my 56th year I was experiencing a complete shift in consciousness. I started to diffuse all communication within the dream in this life. I was at the precipice of a significant and deliberate swing, a readiness to be held in Oneness, engaged in the unified whole. I had stopped practising thoughts that enshrined and celebrated separation.

Experiences with higher dimensions and a new wash of vibrational frequencies, made my thirst for change insatiable, I felt true liberation. Any ideas I may have once had of coming to this dimension to just live and die, were altered forever.

My 57th year was the deepest dive WITHIN. At the time I did not know this was the beginning of the final dissolution of all my belief systems and suffering. I was letting go of my humanity and it was habitually invigorating and excruciating.

As my mind started to investigate subtler states, my sensory perceptions were wholly amplified. I witnessed my individuality initiate forgetting itself.

Experiencing life in this way became effortless, a silent and willing surrender with devotion. I started observing Consciousness falling in Love with itself over and over again. I understood the dissolution of time and space and the entire chronicle of the universe is in the NOW. If God Consciousness is omnipresent then God is permeating every part of me at any given moment and instinctively every part of me started to experience God. I am a Rishi in training, understood in the Vedic world view as an accomplished and enlightened person. My aspiration is to attain Cosmic, God and possibly Unity Consciousness where 'myself is the Self of all'.

With all that I have witnessed in reviewing and healing my life and living in 'Oneness', I feel my purpose is to connect and assist humanity.

To be of loving service to the whole as a conscious giver of the energy labelled as 'Love'. To help dissolve the cyclical sufferance carried by others. To support the coupling of Gaia and her kingdoms and forge an intimate relationship between the cosmos and the individual. I believe I am preparing to ascend, to journey back to Source and return to this life with the wisdom of that loving intelligence and Consciousness, a crystalline remembrance of the purity of One.

On December 21st, 2019, the Gateway for thousands of souls to ascend unlocked, it concretized for many in March of 2020, others, in their own timeline will continue to rise. Humanity is reclaiming its potential to walk amongst the stars.

I am so fortunate to live in Bali, Indonesia where the Female and Male Great Dragon ley lines connect and pass through six sacred sites to assist with purifying the planet, and the custodians of the land offer devotional prayer and ceremony daily. Since the gateway opened, I cannot express the unity I have with this remembrance and the brilliance of the life I am experiencing. To bear witness to this timeless moment is indescribable. I have been humming with accelerated and indescribable frequencies in full effervescence. Like a Cheshire cat on a Magical carpet ride.

Today I feel called to emulate God, to pay homage to something infinitely greater than anything I have ever imagined. This is my Purposeful Truth; I am connected to everything and everyone and we are co-creating a new template for humanity that will surpass anything we have ever known. I am so graced to be here to witness this profound homecoming of collective consciousness.

On the internal horizon a setting sun creates a mystifying outline of what is to come. Finally, I have returned to a peaceful shelter, which I think of as God's home.

God has come, a timeless warmth and removed the harsh shard from my once broken heart.

I exhale and reflect as I bow my head and sway 'shhhhhhhhhhhhhhh...my torn flesh is mended'.

"Our deepest fear is not that we are not inadequate. our deepest fear is that that we are powerful beyond measure."

~ Marianne Williamson

AUTHOR BIOGRAPHIES

———— ❖ ————

Robin Seeger

CHAPTER ONE

Robin loves his role as an "Inner Truth Activator," enabling men and women that work with him to take control of their life while helping them to unlock "their path," releasing blocks and allowing transformation to take place, creating lasting change.

He is a compassionate husband, father of two, intuitive mentor, Shamanic Reiki Healer and published bestselling co-author.

In 2007, he was confronted with a sudden onset of a life-altering illness with symptoms comparable to Multiple Sclerosis.

The following years tested his resilient and determined nature. He was involved in several serious motor vehicle accidents, which redefined his perspective on life.

Overcoming all the symptoms and fully recovering from the accidents through lifestyle changes and a steadily shifting, life-affirming mindset, he took this opportunity to change his life.

Robin retired from a life that looked perfect to the outside world, to reconnect to himself and his family.

He left the safety of his job and the familiar surroundings of Vancouver, Canada, and with his family embarked on a healing journey of reflection and self-discovery, allowing him to find his true calling of being a leader and mentor.

His teachings are shaped by combining his extensive knowledge leading corporate commercial companies, utilizing his logical mind with his innate, intuitive, shamanic nature to navigate easily through challenges of any kind and connect with his clients on a deeper level.

He is now living a life following his passion for facilitating men's and mixed circles, empowerment and parenting workshops, retreats, private mentoring and coaching sessions.

www.truthwarrior.online or instagram.com/sacredrebel

Julie Williams

CHAPTER TWO

J ulie Williams, Healer & Scientist, combines her love of science with extensive training in sacred and holistic healing arts for a powerful combination with a heart-based approach.

She graduated with a degree in Biology and worked in biotechnology and clinical research before changing her career and realizing her true calling as a healer. She developed and currently practices Consciousness Medicine, a natural healing method which integrates multiple holistic therapy certifications, including Family Constellations, Energy Medicine, NLP (Neuro-Linguistic

Programming), Massage, Advanced Yoga, Quantum Healing, Shamanism, and Intuitive Arts.

Inspired by the powerful impact that Family Constellation work had on her own life, Julie became a facilitator in 2005 and has trained at the Hellinger Institute of DC, the University of California Santa Barbara, and NLP Marin. Julie owns her own clinical practice and runs workshops, retreats, and training courses worldwide. Learn more at: www.consciousness-medicine.com.

John Spender

CHAPTER THREE

J ohn Spender is a 20-time International Best Selling co-author, who didn't learn how to read and write at a basic level until he was ten years old. He has since traveled the world and started many businesses leading him to create the best-selling book series *A Journey Of Riches* He is an Award Winning International Speaker and Movie Maker.

John was an international NLP trainer and has coached thousands of people from various backgrounds through all sorts of challenges. From the borderline homeless to very wealthy individuals, he has helped many people to get in touch with their truth to create a life on their terms.

John's search for answers to living a fulfilling life has taken him to work with Native American Indians in the Hills of San Diego, the forests of Madagascar, swimming with humpback whales in Tonga, exploring the Okavango Delta of Botswana and the Great Wall of China. He's traveled from Chile to Slovakia, Hungary to the Solomon Islands, the mountains of Italy and the streets of Mexico.

Everywhere his journey has taken him, John has discovered a hunger among people to find a new way to live, with a yearning for freedom of expression. His belief is that everyone has a book in them.

He is now a writing coach having worked with more than 200 authors from 40 different countries for the *A Journey of Riches* series http://ajourneyofriches.com/ and his publishing house, Motion Media International has published 20 non-fiction titles to date.

He also co-wrote and produced the movie documentary *Adversity* starring Jack Canfield, Rev. Micheal Bernard Beckwith, Dr. John Demartini and many more, coming soon in 2020. Moreover, you can bet there will be a best-selling book to follow! Apply to read in the series here www.ajourneyofriches.com

Lilibeth Ranchez

CHAPTER FOUR

Beth was born and raised in San Antonio, Delfin Albano, Isabela, the northern part of the Philippines.

She is the eldest of five children to her loving parents the late Jaime Ranchez, Senior and Iluminada Macadangdang Ranchez.

She graduated from High School as Valedictorian with two Gold medals and granted a scholarship by the University of the Philippines. She attended Far Eastern University, where she was awarded a full scholarship graduating with a Bachelor of Arts majoring in Economics and top of the National College Entrance Examination (NCEE).

Beth joined the Philippine Armed Forces in the Philippines as a Civilian employee and migrated to Australia during the mid-spring of 1986.

She studied in Financial Planning while working full time with two small kids and worked in the Financial Planning department of the two biggest banks in Australia, Australian & New Zealand Bank (ANZ), then to Commonwealth Bank of Australia (CBA).

Beth is the proud mother of two children. Cristina Ashleigh, who also followed her Mum's profession in the Financial Planning industry. Christopher Blake, who has now finished his double degree in Bachelor of Science in Engineering - Computer Systems Engineer & Computer Science (with honors) early this year.

Beth is also a co-author and writer of book 17 in the *A Journey of Riches* series, *In Search of Happiness* and the 19th book *Building Your Dreams*.

Debi Beebe

CHAPTER FIVE

D ebi Beebe built an extremely successful career in the fitness and nutrition industry for 30 years by being a private trainer to celebrity clientele. She was a fitness model, is a black belt in Tae Kwon Do, and a certified Tae Bo instructor.

After semi-retiring, she discovered a Health and Wellness network marketing company aligned with her values. She became fired up and went to work, helping as many people as she could to increase their health and their wealth globally. She quickly reached millionaire status within the company. Debi made her way to become one of the most powerful women in network marketing, speaking on international stages, and running training's about business and mindset.

Over the years, she realized that empowering people is one of her most essential purposes, starting with our mindset. Debi Beebe is the creator of Manage Your Mindset Monday, a biweekly platform, to mentor upcoming leaders and anyone who wants to achieve more in their life. She truly strives to support others to be difference-makers.

Being a Difference Maker in all areas, and Giving back is one of the most significant ways to show love on a bigger scale. Debi, her husband Jeff, and their adult children and granddaughter give their time and resources to the beloved company's IsaFoundation and The Ronald McDonald House. This is true fulfillment.

"Health is our Wealth, and Wealth is our Health, and the two cannot be divided."

Contact information: debibeebe.me or debibeebe@gmail.com

Marie Crawford

CHAPTER SIX

Marie is a 45-year-old Virginia native and a devoted mother to two remarkable children, who she spends much of her time with to this day. She is also a proud Mimi to a beautiful nine-month-old granddaughter and has four loveable fur babies.

Marie is the Human Resources Manager for a non-profit company that is dedicated to dynamically altering outcomes for at-risk children and their families by delivering services designed to increase resiliency and strengthen relationships. Marie has over 18 years of management and leadership experience, as well as a decade of experience as a tax preparer. Marie is a confident and motivated difference-maker, with excellent communication and organizational skills.

At the age of 40, Marie decided she would start living her best life. She started kickboxing and running 5K and obstacle course races. In September 2020, Marie will run her first half marathon. She became a certified COBRA Self Defense instructor in 2018. Marie is always seeking an adventure; she is interested in investigating the paranormal and loves traveling. Marie is passionate about being outdoors and feels most at peace at the beach and when she is hiking.

Over the past four years, Marie has been focusing on self-development, self-awareness, the forgiveness of herself and others, the power of positivity and releasing negative energy and thoughts. Marie attended a life-changing retreat in 2017 that inspired a shift in self-love and gratitude. Marie desires to help others improve their health and wellness and strives to encourage others on their self-love journey.

Suzanne Rushton

CHAPTER SEVEN

Suzanne Rushton is a Canadian creator, entrepreneur and photographer. Based in Vancouver, a global wanderer at heart, her main goal in life is to be a Bond Woman. She has been reading, writing and capturing thoughts for decades and is scared but excited to share them with you and the world.

You make mistakes. Suzanne has a lot of experience in making mistakes. Her chapter will make you feel better about yours. Her writing is punchy, to the point, and packed with ideas for getting unstuck and laughing about the times that you couldn't.

Despite having a background in Petroleum Engineering, Geology and Geography, Suzanne pivoted and built a photography empire consisting of corporate real estate, prestigious events, and sparkly global travel (maybe that one is for her personal gratification).

Her large-format nature images can be seen on the inside of office buildings filling up entire walls. She also built a photography tourism business that quickly shot to the top ten Vancouver listed activities on Tripadvisor.

So, while she is quirky and self-deprecating in the story, she is actually somewhat productive even during dark days, much to her surprise. Of course, you can see proof of all this on Instagram @suzannerushton.

When she's not building businesses, you can find her doing breath workshops, spinning poi, and trying to make sense of her life.

Ryan Doherty

CHAPTER EIGHT

R yan Doherty was born in a small town in Central Queensland. When he started his electrical apprenticeship, he developed excruciating back pain. Ryan overcame this through exercise, and 18 months later would take a 3rd place in a bodybuilding contest.

When other adversities occurred in life, he found a love of dance and placed 3rd in the beginners category at the nationals for modern jive. Today he is an electrician studying for an associate degree in electrical engineering with a commendation from the

Dean of Engineering and Technology for achieving high distinctions in his first year.

Having studied personal development for ten years, he has recently completed the DreamBuilder program and LifeMastery program with Coach Tamia, a transformational coach and one of the world's highest-ranked Distributors for Enagic.

The greatest loves in his life are his partner of 12 years, a three-year-old son and baby girl on the way.

Annie Pearson

CHAPTER NINE

Annie Pearson, mother, daughter, sister, is founder of Admin Happy and passionate about Human Potential for herself and humanity.

Annie shares her story from having lost all her confidence through a relationship to 'alignment' as she worked to rebuild, consciously create, reconnect and 're align' with her true inner self. In effect, she managed to 'return to love' to the point she felt solid enough as a person to go ahead and have a child on her own by donor at the age of 41

From her experience and personal learning, she is keen to share some tips on what assisted her in 'Returning to Love' 'Alignment.'

Mia Paul

CHAPTER TEN

Mia Paul is an Australian born, Greek Cypriot designer. She has spent her life exploring the increasing elasticity between Art, Architecture, Fashion, Photography and Design. She is the polyamorous lover of all the above talents, a polymath contributor who investigates current opportunities, and revels in the title of spiritual entrepreneur.

Attracting eclectic prospects to keep redefining herself, she is renowned for her progressive and provocative imagery, reflecting a combined simplicity and depth that is instinctive, limitless and stimulating.

"I work with enthusiasm and passion, combining a synthesis of cultural influences with a profound sense of the surreal."

Everything she creates is masterfully structured with opulent details and influenced by diverse urban environments. Her food architecture, fashion and interiors are for the brave, tactile and self-expressive.

She has a devout daily practice of yoga, qigong and meditation, embracing spirituality with enthusiasm, peace and harmony. She envisages humanity growing into an unstoppable tidal wave of Consciousness and Love, resulting in radically reshaping the entire planet so we may become spiritually free and this rests with us.

She notes that discipline and regular practice are vital to becoming more conscious and embracing an awakened state. Mia confirms that she has experienced fear, failure, success and empowerment in equal proportions in her life.

"With the anarchy of a curious child, I source my ideas from a vibrant image bank, stored from years of witnessing the most unexpected. I am always looking

for sacred geometric patterns of energy in design and humanity and support the natural metamorphosis and abundance of all people, places + things."

"**Above all, practice being loyal to your soul.**"

~ John Roger

Afterword

I hope you enjoyed the collection of heartfelt stories, wisdom and vulnerability shared. Storytelling is the oldest form of communication, and I hope you feel inspired to take a step toward living a fulfilling life. Feel free to contact any of the authors in this book, or the other books in this series.

The proceeds of this book will go to feeding many of the rural Balinese families that are struggling through the current pandemic.

Other books in the series are...

Develop Inner Strength : *A Journey of Riches,* Book Twenty
https://www.amazon.com/dp/1925919153

Building your Dreams : A Journey of Riches, Book Nineteen
https://www.amazon.com/dp/B081KZCN5R

Liberate your Struggles : A Journey of Riches, Book Eighteen
https://www.amazon.com/dp/1925919099

In Search of Happiness : A Journey of Riches, Book
Seventeen
https://www.amazon.com/dp/B07R8HMP3K

Tapping into Courage : A Journey of Riches, Book
Sixteen
https://www.amazon.com/dp/B07NDCY1KY

The Power Healing : A Journey of Riches, Book Fifteen
https://www.amazon.com/dp/B07LGRJQ2S

The Way of the Entrepreneur: A Journey Of Riches, Book
Fourteen
https://www.amazon.com/dp/B07KNHYR8V

Discovering Love and Gratitude: A Journey Of Riches,
Book Thirteen
https://www.amazon.com/dp/B07H23Q6D1

Transformational Change: A Journey Of Riches, Book
Twelve
https://www.amazon.com/dp/B07FYHMQRS

Finding Inspiration: A Journey Of Riches, Book Eleven
https://www.amazon.com/dp/B07F1LS1ZW

*Building your Life from Rock Bottom: A Journey Of
Riches,* Book Ten
https://www.amazon.com/dp/B07CZK155Z

Transformation Calling: A Journey Of Riches, Book Nine
https://www.amazon.com/dp/B07BWQY9FB

Letting Go and Embracing the New: A Journey Of Riches, Book Eight
https://www.amazon.com/dp/B079ZKT2C2

Making Empowering Choices: A Journey Of Riches, Book Seven
https://www.amazon.com/Making-Empowering-Choices-Journey-Riches-ebook/dp/B078JXMK5V

The Benefit of Challenge: A Journey Of Riches, Book Six
https://www.amazon.com/dp/B0778S2VBD

Personal Changes: A Journey Of Riches, Book Five
https://www.amazon.com/dp/B075WCQM4N

Dealing with Changes in Life: A Journey Of Riches, Book Four
https://www.amazon.com/dp/B0716RDKK7

Making Changes: A Journey Of Riches, Book Three
https://www.amazon.com/dp/B01MYWNI5A

The Gift In Challenge: A Journey Of Riches, Book Two
https://www.amazon.com/dp/B01GBEML4G

From Darkness into the Light: A Journey Of Riches, Book One
https://www.amazon.com/dp/B018QMPHJW

Thank you to all the authors that have shared aspects of their lives in the hope that it will inspire others to live a bigger version of themselves. I heard a great saying from Jim Rohan, "You can't complain and feel grateful at the same time." At any given moment, we have a choice to either feel like a victim of life, or be connected and grateful for it. I hope this book helps you to feel grateful, and go after your dreams. For more information about contributing to the series, visit http://ajourneyofriches.com/ . Furthermore if you enjoyed reading this book, we would appreciate your review on Amazon to help get our message out to more people.